Preface

This book represents the text of the O'Donnell Lectures in Celtic Studies delivered in the University of Oxford in May 1983. There were originally three lectures, the first forming the substance of Chapters 1 and 2 here, the second Chapters 3 and 4, and the third Chapters 5 and 6. The essence of my original comments remains, although the section on the English was reworked for talks in Kalamazoo in 1987 and at the Anglo-American Conference of Historians in London in the same year. The whole book has also been able to benefit from some excellent work that has come to light in the six years since the lectures were first written.

Though this is intended as an independent work, the ideas in it arose from writing a general book about early medieval Wales in the period 1979–82, and the lectures were a further exploration of matters too lengthy and too specialized to deal with in a book for the general reader. Too intricate and difficult, too, although I have now tried to make the subject intelligible to those with little background and have referred throughout to translations of the crucial texts. But my treatment is intentionally discursive: this is an *exploration* of ideas about power in early Wales, not a comprehensive survey of it. I remain extremely grateful, as I was in 1983, to the Board of Electors to the Lectureship for allowing me the opportunity to indulge and explore, and I remain conscious of the honour in the invitation.

I am glad to record my thanks to Leicester University Press for permission to use Fig. 32 from my *Wales in the Early Middle Ages* (1982), and to David Hill for permission to use his map of Offa's and Wat's Dykes (especially for his personal interest in ensuring that I had an up-to-date model), as also to Colin Stuart for drawing the maps and figures, and to Eva Wilson for the jacket drawing. Particular thanks are also due to Ellis Evans, who was my host at the Oxford occasions, and to the friends who have read draft chapters since—to James Graham-Campbell, Morfydd Owen, Patrick Wormald, and especially to Huw Pryce who has read most. As ever, if I have not taken their advice, it is my fault not theirs. I should also like to record my gratitude to the friends who supplied me with books and photocopies at a time when a very Welsh disease made it difficult to get about.

W.D.

Bucknell
September 1989

*Patterns of Power
in Early Wales*

PATTERNS OF POWER IN EARLY WALES

WENDY DAVIES

O'Donnell Lectures
delivered in the University of Oxford
1983

CLARENDON PRESS · OXFORD
1990

Oxford University Press, Walton Street, Oxford OX2 6DP

Oxford New York Toronto
Delhi Bombay Calcutta Madras Karachi
Petaling Jaya Singapore Hong Kong Tokyo
Nairobi Dar es Salaam Cape Town
Melbourne Auckland
and associated companies in
Berlin Ibadan

Oxford is a trade mark of Oxford University Press

Published in the United States
by Oxford University Press, New York

British Library Cataloguing in Publication Data
Davies, Wendy
Patterns of power in early Wales.
1. Wales, 1066–1399
I. Title
942.902
ISBN 0–19–820153–2

Library of Congress Cataloging in Publication Data
Davies, Wendy.
Patterns of power in early Wales / Wendy Davies.
p.   cm.
Includes bibliographical references.
1. Wales—History—To 1536.   2. Wales—Politics and government.
I. Title.
DA715.D375 1990
942.9—dc20   90–30873
ISBN 0–19–820153–2

Typeset by Pentacor PLC, High Wycombe, Bucks

Printed and bound in
Great Britain by Bookcraft Ltd.
Midsomer Norton, Bath

For my father

Contents

List of Figures

Plates

Abbreviations

Book of Llan Dâv: *The Text of the Book of Llan Dâv*, ed. J. G. Evans with J. Rhys (Oxford, 1893).

De excidio: Gildas, *De excidio et conquestu Britanniae*, in *Chronica Minora saec. IV. V. VI. VII*, 3, ed. T. Mommsen (MGH AA 13; Berlin, 1898).

ECMW: V. E. Nash-Williams, *The Early Christian Monuments of Wales* (Cardiff, 1950).

Vita Cadoci: in *Vitae Sanctorum Britanniae et Genealogiae*, ed. A. W. Wade-Evans (Cardiff, 1944), 24–140.

1. The Problem

This is a book about power, concepts of it, and practice of it, in Wales in the early middle ages. It is cast as an investigation—an exploration—of the nature of political authority in pre-Conquest Wales. That so familiar a concept should need exploration may seem surprising, but defining and describing power is itself a problem in such poorly evidenced, rural communities as we find in medieval western Britain. What *was* 'power' in western Britain? What did it mean to have power and be powerful? These questions are fundamental—easy to pose, difficult to answer, but unavoidable. They naturally involve consideration of the distribution of power, both territorially and socially, and such changes in that distribution as may be perceived; they must also involve consideration of the way people thought about power; they will inevitably extend to problems of legitimacy, of the acceptable limits of action, and of the status of the individual, besides issues of practical politics like internal competition and foreign influence.

Past treatment, and past avoidance, of this subject has become increasingly irritating: twentieth-century writers on early Wales seem to have a very limited appreciation of the ways power could be distributed in an early medieval society. An all-purpose 'lord' and 'lordship', particularly favoured by translators of the vernacular, are liberally scattered through these works without any attempt to spell out, let alone question, the user's assumptions about the meaning of the terms; indeed, their use suggests analogies with political systems elsewhere in medieval Europe, although any clarification of the nature and limits of the analogy is strikingly absent.[1] So, too, we find words like 'overkingship' and 'overlordship' tossed about with no attempt to investigate the nature of the dependence implied, nor the relationship

---

[1] See S. Reynolds, *Kingdoms and Communities in Western Europe, 900–1300* (Oxford, 1984), *passim* and 219 especially.

between 'overperson' and 'underperson'. Although we often cannot locate the territorial base of political authority, assumptions about the political implications of territorial conquest, as also of migration and settlement, are commonplace. Essential questions have to be posed here: in what circumstances did military victory have subsequent political implications? (We cannot assume that it always had any.) What precisely were those implications and how did they vary? and how dependent were they on associated migration and settlement? Was a victory only significant if settlers filled in behind it? Conversely, we need to spell out the question: at what point, if at all, did English or Irish or Viking settlement imply political domination? and we have to consider it before assuming that the presence of aliens in an area necessarily meant rule of it, or its inhabitants, by those aliens. Furthermore, these issues are easily confused with issues of property rights, for the arrival of aliens need mean no more than new landlords or new free peasants; but ownership of landed property might well bring control of resident labour as well as regular income and we therefore need to confront another question: when and where and in what senses was the landlord 'ruler' of his property?

Problems of power, then, are inextricably associated with military activity and with rulership, but also with population movement and with landlordship. Some aspects of these problems in Wales have of course been confronted; there is the problem symbolized by the use of the word *gwlad* ('country'): was this unit merely hypothetical or was it, as Sir John Lloyd maintained, the ancestor of the late medieval administrative *cantref*, a physical entity and a real political unit? Was it identifiable with a notional *tud*, 'population group', Lloyd's 'body of free tribesmen'? In other words, in the early medieval past were there tribal communities and if so did they have a political as well as a social identity—was each 'tribe' a 'country', a political unit?[2] There is also the terminological problem associated with the word *brenin*, meaning 'person of status' and signifying 'king' from the twelfth century onwards:

---

[2] J. E. Lloyd, *A History of Wales from the Earliest Times to the Edwardian Conquest* (London, 1911), 302.

why was it *this* word that was used for 'king' rather than *rhi*, a word which existed in Old Welsh and which might have been expected by comparison with Irish usage and with the cognate Irish *rí*, 'king'? Does the implied shift in the terminology of high political authority from *rhi* to *brenin* imply some change in political structures too?[3] There is also J. G. Edwards's influential suggestion that in the course of the Norman Conquest the conquerors took over a local aristocracy's existing political powers, powers which were defined with reference to units called commotes, and thereby neither imposed nor developed structures and institutions of their own. Though study of the Conquest during the past decade has considerably refined this suggestion, it still has reverberations in works on the early middle ages.[4] These are separable questions but they relate to the fundamental problems and need framing in the context of an overall enquiry. We need to investigate the distinction—if there was one—between power over men and power over land; and that—if there was one—between power over property and power over a 'rulerdom'; and we have to assess how far they coincided. We need to investigate the varying qualities of power over men, if such there were, and of power over land, as well as their inter-relationships.

In fact, although the key questions are ultimately about practical capacities, they are initially terminological. We have to begin by considering what we mean, and what contemporaries meant, by the terms of rule, power, and dominance that they used. Whatever the terms, however, in the end the central question must be what did rule involve—what could (and did) rulers do—was everyone ruled—were the powers of rule focused on single individuals or dispersed through an aristocracy or a hierarchy—and hence, if notions like overkingship

[3] T. M. Charles-Edwards, 'Native Political Organization in Roman Britain and the Origin of MW *brenhin*', in *Antiquitates Indogermanicae*, ed. M. Mayrhofer, W. Meid, B. Schlerath, R. Schmitt (Innsbruck, 1974).
[4] J. G. Edwards, 'The Normans and the Welsh March', *Proc. British Academy*, 42 (1956); the problem has essentially been dealt with by R. R. Davies, 'Kings, Lords and Liberties in the March of Wales, 1066–1272', *Trans. Royal Historical Society*, 29 (1979), but there are also instructive comments on the complexity of the issue in I. W. Rowlands, 'The Making of the March: Aspects of the Norman Settlement in Dyfed', in *Proc. Battle Conference 3, 1980*, ed. R. A. Brown (Woodbridge, 1981), 152–4.

were appropriate, were they to do with distinctive and peculiar powers or merely with ideas of status?

The problems of this subject do not merely lie in the early medievalist's reluctance to frame sufficiently probing questions. It is a problematic area in other ways since we cannot get away from the fact that the sources for early medieval Wales are poor. They are poor because they are few, largely preserved in late manuscripts, sometimes unintelligible, if not corrupt, and mostly unprovenanced; we know hardly anything about authorship. Hence, and it is essential to be honest about this, there is very little that can be conclusively demonstrated; most aspects of most interpretations are arguable. For that very reason Sir John Lloyd's interpretation of early Welsh political development, which has dominated all consideration of pre- and post-Norman Conquest politics since the early twentieth century, needs questioning; for the pre-Conquest period, at least, he set up an apparently immovable framework. Without intending any disrespect to Lloyd—who was undoubtedly one of the century's great historians—we have to recognize that other frameworks and other interpretations are possible. We can make different patterns with the pieces.[5]

Although limited in quality and quantity, the nature of the available source material is very varied. Given the corruptions and difficulties of the manuscript evidence, the corpus of inscribed stones from Wales—occasionally still *in situ*—is of exceptional importance; and, given these problems, the increasing corpus of archaeological material has especial value: it is localizable, and quantifiable, and is almost the only source of new data.[6] As for the character of the manuscript evidence, it

[5] Lloyd, *History of Wales*. But for the period from the Norman Conquest, see now R. R. Davies, *Conquest, Coexistence, and Change: Wales 1063–1415* (Oxford, 1987).

[6] V. E. Nash-Williams, *The Early Christian Monuments of Wales* (Cardiff, 1950); new stones still come to light: see, for example, J. Knight and others, 'New Finds of Early Christian Monuments', *Archaeologia Cambrensis*, 126 (1977); the entire corpus is in the course of revision and republication by the Royal Commission on Historical Monuments. For archaeology, see the annual reports of the Council for British Archaeology, *Archaeology in Wales*; and for a particularly useful recent collection, *Early Medieval Settlements in Wales AD 400–1100*, ed. N. Edwards and A. Lane (Bangor and Cardiff, 1988).

is sometimes written in Latin and sometimes in the vernacular. The Latin material includes annals (Irish and Welsh), the Welsh Annals perhaps being local to St David's from the late eighth century until after the Norman Conquest.[7] There are also charters, overwhelmingly from the South-East, running from the very late sixth to the eleventh century, although the earliest texts are extremely corrupt; and there are narrative pieces, like the *Historia Brittonum* of the early ninth century, Asser's Life of the English king Alfred of the late ninth, and the unprovenanced tract of the early sixth century written by Gildas, on the miserable state of politics and contemporary society.[8] There are also Saints' Lives: seventh- and ninth-century Breton Lives and eleventh-century Welsh ones;[9] there are penitential materials, probably of the sixth and seventh centuries, a few scholarly writings—like the ninth- or tenth-century Colloquy of Oxoniensis Posterior (Bodleian MS 572 (of

[7] *Annales Cambriae*, ed. J. Williams ab Ithel (Rolls Series; London, 1860); see K. Hughes, 'The Welsh Latin Chronicles: *Annales Cambriae* and Related Texts', *Proc. British Academy*, 69 (1973), and D. N. Dumville's review, *Studia Celtica*, 12–13 (1977–8), 461–7. Hughes argued for the St David's provenance from the late eighth century; I have doubts that it was this early, since there is very little Dyfed material in the Annals before the later tenth century, as also Dumville in K. Grabowski and D. Dumville, *Chronicles and Annals of Mediaeval Ireland and Wales* (Woodbridge, 1984), 207–26; see further below, p. 40 n. 12. For Irish Annals see *The Annals of Ulster (to AD 1131)*, ed. S. Mac Airt and G. Mac Niocaill (Dublin, 1983).

[8] Charters principally in *The Text of the Book of Llan Dâv*, ed. J. G. Evans with J. Rhys (Oxford, 1893); see W. Davies, *The Llandaff Charters* (Aberystwyth, 1979). *Historia Brittonum*: *Chronica Minora saec. IV. V. VI. VII*, 3, ed. T. Mommsen (MGH AA 13; Berlin, 1898); see D. Dumville, ' "Nennius" and the *Historia Brittonum*', *Studia Celtica*, 10–11 (1975–6); id., 'The Corpus Christi "Nennius" ', *Bulletin of the Board of Celtic Studies*, 25 (1972–4); id., 'Some Aspects of the Chronology of the *Historia Brittonum*', ibid. *Asser's Life of King Alfred*, ed. W. H. Stevenson (Oxford, 1904); see *Alfred the Great*, trans. S. Keynes and M. Lapidge (Harmondsworth, 1983), 48–58. Gildas, *De excidio et conquestu Britanniae*: *Chronica Minora*, 3, ed. Mommsen; see *Gildas: New Approaches*, ed. M. Lapidge and D. Dumville (Woodbridge, 1984).

[9] *Vitae Sanctorum Britanniae et Genealogiae*, ed. and trans. A. W. Wade-Evans (Cardiff, 1944); see K. Hughes, 'British Museum MS. Cotton Vespasian A. xiv ('*Vitae Sanctorum Wallensium*'): Its Purpose and Provenance', in N. Chadwick and others, *Studies in the Early British Church* (Cambridge, 1958), and W. Davies, 'Property Rights and Property Claims in Welsh "Vitae" of the Eleventh Century', in *Hagiographie, cultures et sociétés*, ed. E. Patlagean and P. Riché (Paris, 1981). *La Vie de S. Samson*, ed. R. Fawtier (Paris, 1912); see I. N. Wood, 'Forgery in Merovingian Hagiography', in *Fälschungen im Mittelalter*, 5 (Hanover, 1988) (= MGH Schriften 33. 5).

Brittonic if not Welsh provenance)), poems of the late eleventh century, and one martyrology of the same period.[10]

The vernacular material includes some fragmentary or very brief bits and pieces, like the ninth-century charters in the Lichfield Gospels, computistical writings, and the small but extremely important corpus of glosses on the works of classical and later Latin literature (not just Ovid but later writers like Juvencus and Martianus Capella feature too).[11] However, by far the most important aspect of the vernacular material is the poetry. This is exceptionally difficult to use because its chronological context (not to mention its geographical context) is very insecure. Although some of the content of these poems and even some of their formulation may be of seventh-century—or late sixth-century—origin, our present written texts are in thirteenth-century or later manuscripts and cannot be copies of written versions of pre-ninth-century origin. Nevertheless, poems which have more and poems which have fewer archaic characteristics are distinguishable and this gives some sense, however imperfect, of relative chronology; of the earlier, the texts established by Sir Ifor Williams—*Canu Aneirin, Canu Taliesin*, and *Canu Llywarch Hen*—represent sets of poems which could well derive from ninth-century written texts, and there is a strong body of opinion that would see a pre-ninth-century oral origin for *Canu Aneirin* and *Canu Taliesin*. A few poems have been associated with a particular though not very closely dated chronological context—*Armes Prydein*, of the early to mid-tenth century, is the best example—and these are especially useful.[12] The vernacular

[10] *The Irish Penitentials*, ed. L. Bieler (Dublin, 1963), 60–72; see W. Davies, *Wales in the Early Middle Ages* (Leicester, 1982), 204. M. Lapidge, 'Latin Learning in Dark Age Wales', in *Proc. of the Seventh International Congress of Celtic Studies*, ed. D. E. Evans, J. G. Griffith, E. M. Jope (Oxford, 1986). M. Lapidge, 'The Welsh-Latin Poetry of Sulien's family', *Studia Celtica*, 8–9 (1973–4), 78–92; see ibid. 68–78, and Davies, *Wales*, 212–14.

[11] *Book of Llan Dâv*, ed. Evans with Rhys, pp. xliii–xlvii. W. Stokes, 'The Welsh Glosses and Verses in the Cambridge Codex of Juvencus', *Trans. Philological Society* (1860–1); id., 'The Old-Welsh Glosses on Martianus Capella, with Some Notes on the Juvencus-Glosses', *Beiträge zur vergleichenden Sprachforschung*, ed. A. Kuhn, 7 (Berlin, 1873); see Davies, *Wales*, 202 and 213.

[12] *Canu Aneirin*, ed. I. Williams (Cardiff, 1938); *Canu Taliesin*, ed. I. Williams (Cardiff, 1960); *Canu Llywarch Hen*, ed. I. Williams (Cardiff, 1935), but see also J. Rowland, 'A Study of the Saga Englynion', Ph.D. thesis (3 vols.;

material also includes Welsh translations of the Annals made in the thirteenth century, known as *Brut y Tywysogyon*; these sometimes include material additional to that of our extant Annals, especially for the tenth and eleventh centuries, and this material appears to be translated from some lost Latin sources.[13] I would add that there are also some genealogical collections, largely of names, without comment; the principal collection of early reference is that in British Library Harleian MS 3859, of mid-tenth-century origin, but there is also some genealogical material in narratives like the *Historia Brittonum* and—exceptionally—on the lengthily inscribed stone near Llangollen, the Pillar of Eliseg.[14] There are as one might expect relevant sources from outside Wales: the *Ecclesiastical History* of the Englishman Bede, Irish martyrologies, the English *Domesday Book*, for example; they contribute useful fragments but little more than an occasional different perspective.[15]

The chronological and spatial limits of this study are broad: although it ranges over the period between the fifth and eleventh centuries, inclusive, it will however concentrate on the ninth century and later, for that is the best evidenced in a poorly evidenced era, and that is where there is still matter to explore. The study is also essentially concerned with the area defined by the modern boundary of Wales. However, I shall

University of Wales, 1982), pt. 2 (= vol. 3); *Armes Prydein*, ed. I. Williams, trans. R. Bromwich (Dublin, 1972); see D. Dumville, 'Brittany and "Armes Prydein Vawr" ', *Études Celtiques*, 20 (1983). See Davies, *Wales*, 209–11, for a quick guide, and A. O. H. Jarman, *Aneirin: Y Gododdin* (Welsh Classics, 3; Llandysul, 1988), pp. lxviii–lxxv, for a recent discussion of chronological problems.

[13] *Brut y Tywysogyon, Red Book of Hergest Version*, ed. and trans. T. Jones (Cardiff, 1955); *Brut y Tywysogyon, Peniarth MS. 20*, ed. T. Jones (Cardiff, 1941), which is translated as *Brut y Tywysogyon, Peniarth MS. 20 Version*, trans. T. Jones (Cardiff, 1952). See the very full critical apparatus to these volumes, and also Hughes, 'Welsh Latin Chronicles', *Proc. Brit. Acad.*, 69 (1973).

[14] P. C. Bartrum (ed.), *Early Welsh Genealogical Tracts* (Cardiff, 1966).

[15] *Bede's Ecclesiastical History of the English People*, ed. and trans. B. Colgrave and R. A. B. Mynors (Oxford, 1969); *The Martyrology of Oengus the Culdee*, ed. W. Stokes (Henry Bradshaw Society, 29; 1905); *The Martyrology of Tallaght*, ed. R. I. Best and H. J. Lawlor (Henry Bradshaw Society, 68; 1931); *Domesday Book*, ed. A. Farley (1783). See Davies, *Wales*, 198–218, for fuller comment on all these texts and further references.

make reference to Old Breton and Old Cornish glosses; since Old Breton, Old Cornish, and Old Welsh must have been mutually intelligible, and were scarcely separate languages, it is not unreasonable to consider linguistic evidence for terminology from a wider territory than Wales.[16] So too, although Wales is the focus of the investigation, Irish, English, and Scandinavian people had interests in Wales in the ninth, tenth, and eleventh centuries: we therefore have to consider more than the Welsh to understand Wales and Welsh politics.

[16] K. Jackson, *Language and History in Early Britain* (Edinburgh, 1953), 18–25, and B. L. Olsen and O. J. Padel, 'A Tenth-Century List of Cornish Parochial Saints', *Cambridge Medieval Celtic Studies*, 12 (1986), 40. See now the interesting approach of J. T. Koch, 'The Cynfeirdd Poetry and the Language of the Sixth Century', in *Early Welsh Poetry*, ed. B. F. Roberts (Aberystwyth, 1988).

2. Concepts

We have to begin this exploration of power with words and approaches, with a consideration of the terms of power in use in sixth- to eleventh-century Wales, and of ideas about it. I am concerned here with ways of looking at power, not so much *my* way but *their* way in the early middle ages. This is not easy to investigate: there are no political treatises and scarcely an illuminating narrative comment. The nearest we come to the latter is a passage on Britons and Saxons in the unprovenanced Colloquy in Bodleian MS 572: this maintains that God gave victory to the Britons against the Saxons and did so because they were poor and humble, an ideology as much of 'might does not necessarily triumph' as of God disposes; the text also envisages a hierarchical system of administration, through elders (*patricii*, glossed *hinham*) who sat with the king in council, down to *duces*, then *comites*, then *tribuni*, and finally to *decani*—the lowest members of the hierarchy and in charge of ten men each; there are hints of some knowledge of the late Roman administrative system in this, with local elaborations like the *tribunus* in charge of two settlements or *trefi* (*tribus* or *villa* in Latin).[1] There are undoubtedly ideas here, but the passage is garbled and the context insecure. In the absence of explicit theorizing, the best that we can do is look at words used of rule and rulers, in order to throw some light on concepts of power. In this it is obviously more important to identify prevailing trends and tendencies than to deal with exceptions and isolated examples.

[1] *Early Scholastic Colloquies*, ed. W. H. Stevenson (Oxford, 1929), 1. 9, sect. 24; see Lapidge, 'Latin Learning', in *Proc. Seventh Internat. Cong. Celt. Stud.*, ed. Evans and others, 94–7, whose comments suggest that a ninth- or tenth-century date may be appropriate for this passage. In its schematic and partly territorial approach, the passage is not unlike the fiscal models of the Welsh law texts. See D. Jenkins, *The Law of Hywel Dda* (Llandysul, 1986), 121; compare the use made of this schema by G. R. J. Jones, 'Post-Roman Wales', in *The Agrarian History of England and Wales*, 1, pt. 2, ed. H. P. R. Finberg (Cambridge, 1972), 299–304, and id., 'Multiple Estates and Early Settlement', in *Medieval Settlement*, ed. P. H. Sawyer (London, 1976), as also many other of his publications. See further below, p. 82 n. 4.

TERMS FOR RULERS

It is perfectly clear from the terms available and from the context of their use that notions of rule and rulers existed in early medieval Wales: in other words, people thought that powers of command, direction, control, and constraint were monopolized by a few individuals. So,

> The stewards will collect their taxes . . .
> oppressive rule will give rise to sorrow . . .

or

There was a wicked and tyrannical king called Benlli . . . it was a rule with that tyrant that anyone who had not arrived at his fortress for work by sunrise should be killed.[2]

The idea of rule is more frequently expressed in 'ruler' than in 'rule' words and there are many, perhaps surprisingly many, terms used for ruler; the fact that there is a range of terms, and that they are used in different ways, is itself significant. Latin writers, however, have an overwhelming preference for a single ruler word—*rex*, 'king'; we find this throughout annals, Saints' Lives, inscriptions, charters, and narratives. So prevalent is it that we even find *rex* used of Roman emperors, in ninth-century texts like the *Historia Brittonum*, and in the inscription on the Pillar of Eliseg, as well as in other genealogies and in the work of Gildas.

Although the word *rex* is overwhelmingly predominant, the words used to qualify it and the contexts of its use suggest that *reges* could be of different grades; hence, Maelgwn the 'great king', *magnus rex*, among *reges*, and Ambrosius 'king of all kings', *rex inter omnes reges*, in the *Historia Brittonum*; we even find 'wisest and most renowned of kings', *rex sapientissimus opinatissimus omnium regum*, on the seventh-century inscribed stone commemorating Cadfan. At the other end of the scale come *reguli*, 'little kings'.[3]

---

[2] *Armes Prydein*, lines 21, 38: 'Meiryon eu tretheu dychynnullyn . . . dychyfroy etgyllaeth pennaeth lletfer'; *Historia Brittonum*, cc. 32, 33: 'Erat quidam rex iniquus atque tyrannus valde . . . mos erat apud nequissimum tyrannum, nisi quis ante solis ortum pervenisset ad servitutem in arce interficiebatur.'

[3] *Historia Brittonum*, cc. 48, 62; cf. *De excidio*, ch. 33; *ECMW*, nos. 182, 13.

Where *rex* is not used, the numerically significant exceptions are of two types: first, *dux* in the singular, 'duke' or
'leader', is used specifically to designate English royal officers
as also some other people with a military following; so, the
English *dux* Aelfhere led a band of ravaging Saxons in 983, or a
dux Sawyl raided south-east Wales with his cronies, or the
hero Arthur was described as *dux bellorum*, 'war leader'.[4]
The second type of alternative Latin usage involves words like
seniores, meliores, and *optimates,* in the plural, 'elders' or
'worthies', who deliberated and acted as a group: the elders of
Ergyng witnessed property transactions in the mid-eighth
century; and Hengest and King Vortigern consulted with their
elders before taking political action.[5] Less common words
include *dominus,* 'master', 'owner', 'lord', which is very rare
before the late eleventh century; *protictor,* surely a translation
of the vernacular, occurs uniquely on the Castell Dwyran
stone, used of the sixth-century Dyfed ruler Voteporix; wicked
tyrants—*tyranni*—appear here and there, and are always
presented as wicked, unlike the local *tiranni* (machtierns) of
contemporary Brittany; while the *Historia Brittonum* and
Gildas also allow, as well as *reges,* some 'emperors', 'consuls',
and 'patricians' of imperial Rome (*imperatores, consules,
patricii*).[6]

It is very noticeable that despite its general prevalence the
term *rex,* and indeed all ruler words, are strikingly absent from
the late tenth- and early eleventh-century sections of the
Welsh Annals: *rex* is used only once of Welsh kings between
949 and 1018 and no other term is substituted for it in that
period, a time when the recording source was clearly in south-
west Wales; between 949 and 1018 it was usual to refer to
Welsh rulers as N son of N, without descriptive label—'Hywel
ab Ieuaf fought a battle' rather than 'King Hywel fought it' or

---

[4] *Annales Cambriae,* 983, cf. 992; *Vita Cadoci,* ch. 16, cf. ch. 22; *Historia
Brittonum,* ch. 56, cf. ch. 24; *De excidio,* ch. 33.
[5] *Book of Llan Dâv,* nos. 184, 185; cf. ibid., nos. 255, 190a, 198b, 218, 240;
Historia Brittonum, cc. 37, 45; cf. ibid., ch. 40.
[6] *ECMW,* no. 138. *Historia Brittonum,* cc. 31, 32, 33; *De excidio,* cc. 23, 28,
33, etc.; for machtierns see W. Davies, *Small Worlds: The Village Community
in Early Medieval Brittany* (London, 1988), 138–42, and J. G. T. Sheringham,
'Les machtierns', *Mémoires de la société d'histoire et d'archéologie de
Bretagne,* 58 (1981). *Historia Brittonum,* cc. 24, 29, 30.

'Hywel king of Gwynedd'. By contrast, in the eighth- and ninth-century Annals there are frequent references to *reges*, often associated with named regions; and in the later eleventh and twelfth centuries *rex* was used again in the Annals to refer to English, Scottish, and some Welsh kings, and *maximus rex* to an Irish overking, although N son of N was still used a lot for Welsh rulers; in this period Norman lords were called *duces* and *comites*. This is a real hiatus in annalistic practice and the Llandaff charters to some extent echo it: there are few people called *reges* in the late tenth century but more again from the 1020s.[7] We can also observe that later eleventh-, as also twelfth-, century sources used a much greater range of terms for rulers—*dux* ('duke'), *princeps* ('prince'), *regulus* ('little king'), *subregulus* ('subking'), *satraps* ('governor'). This is demonstrated particularly well by the mid-eleventh-century usage of one of the Llandaff records, of 1059: 'if any *rex* or *dux* or *satraps* or *princeps* or any powerful man (*prepotens*) observe this blessing'; but later annals and Saints' Lives do the same.[8]

Vernacular sources, in contrast to the Latin, use a great variety of ruler terms. The bulk of the vernacular source material is poetry and the nature of the source must in some measure explain the fact that there is such a range: poets search for synonyms, and for colourful terms, because they are concerned with style and imagery, and they may use archaic words or coin new ones. Ruler words in the poetry range from words whose principal elements mean in origin 'head' (*unben*, *pennaeth*, *arbennig*) through those meaning 'fighter' (*iud*, *ior*) through those meaning 'leader' (*tywysog*) and those meaning 'supporter' or 'protector' (*kynnelw*, *neirthiad*) to others playing on the analogy of steering, 'rudder', 'helmsman' (*rhwyfadur*, *rhwyf*, *llyw*),[9] as well as terms of rule like *rhi*, *teyrn*, and *gwledig*. Hence,

> he the ruler (*arbennig*), the supreme ruler (*wledic*), the mighty hero;

and

---

[7] *Annales Cambriae*, 1072, 1081, 1093, 1119, etc.; *Book of Llan Dâv*, nos. 249a, 249b, 251, 253, 255, 257, etc.

[8] Ibid. 266.

[9] Cf. Latin *gubernator*, 'governor', 'steersman'.

son of a rightful king, ruler (*ud*) of the men of Gwynedd; . . . Urfai ruler (*ud*) of Eidyn;

and

> may [St] Dewi be the leader (*tywysog*) of our warriors;

and

> Cynan . . . ruler (*neirthiat*) of a wide dominion;

and

> [Tudfwlch] for your loyal deeds you truly are called the ruler (*rector*),
> the prince (*rwyfadur*);
>
> he is Urien, famous ruler (*eineuyd*) . . .true ruler (*rwyf*) of Christians;

and

> as rulers (*teyrned*) whose possession is [by the right of] descent;
> God (*i ri*) who made heaven and earth.[10]

Despite the number of words used, the ways in which they are used make it abundantly clear that there were rulers of greater and lesser status, just as there are greater and lesser *reges*, and other than *reges*, in the Latin texts; further, that some rulers directed or led others. So, in the poems of *Canu Aneirin* and *Canu Taliesin* there are those that we might describe as 'top' rulers—the *mynawg*, the *gwledig*, the *rhwyfadur*; these words occur in the singular; the rulers they describe direct others (like the *arbenhic teyrned*, 'ruler of rulers') and they have a wide range of associated qualities—fame, wisdom, generosity, moderation, as well as a way of winning battles.[11] There are also lesser rulers, *teyrn*, *rhi*, *brenin*, *iud*, *unben*, and so on; these words frequently occur in the plural and the group of lesser rulers may be led by a pre-eminent one: slaughter in front of 300 *unben*, many *teyrned* in conflict, the warrior

[10] *Canu Taliesin*, 3. 7: 'Ac ef yn arbennic, yn oruchel wledic . . . yn keimyat kynteic'; *Canu Aneirin*, 87b, 100: 'mab brenhin teithiauc. ud gwyndyt', 'ut eidin uruei'; *Armes Prydein*, line 196: 'poet tywyssawc Dewi yr kynifwyr'; *Canu Taliesin*, 1. 23: 'nerthi athwlat lydan'; *Canu Aneirin*, 63d: 'enwir yt elwir oth gywir weithret rector [a Latin borrowing] rwyfyadur'; *Canu Taliesin*, 2. 3, 5: 'Vryen hwn anwawt eineuyd . . . rwysc enwir rwyf bedyd'; *Armes Prydein*, line 14: 'Teyrned a bonhed eu gorescyn'; ibid., line 195: 'i ri a grewys nef ac elwyd'.

[11] *Canu Taliesin*, 2. 2, and 3. 7, 26; ibid., 3. 1–6, 24–6; *Canu Aneirin*, 66a, 68, 75a, 85, 100.

Tafloew fighting in the presence of several *teyrned,* and the glorious *rieu* (plural) of Rheged.[12] At the least the words chosen in these 'early' poems to signify the best of rulers are different, and consistently different, from those chosen to signify the normal run of rulers. The vernacular idiom for 'ruler of rulers' is *arbenhic teyrned* rather than *rex regum.*

In fact there is a distinction between the practice of *Canu Aneirin* and *Canu Taliesin* on the one hand and on the other of *Canu Llywarch Hen* and poems like *Armes Prydein.* We still find a broadly consistent distinction between 'top' ruler words and qualities and those of 'lesser' rulers. But, in the latter group (*CLlH,* and others), the 'top' ruler words of *Canu Aneirin/Canu Taliesin* either do not appear or feature very infrequently; moreover, some of the rarer words of the first group, words like *tywysog* and *arglwydd,* appear more often; and some words of lesser import in *Canu Aneirin* and *Canu Taliesin* acquire greater import: in this the highlighted use of *teyrn* is especially notable, but also increasingly *brenin.* A ruler's court in *Canu Llywarch Hen* is *llys vrenhin.*[13]

Although, as I have indicated, it is extremely difficult to specify the chronological contexts of the poems' composition, it is the common view that the former group—*Canu Aneirin* and *Canu Taliesin*—have more archaic elements than the latter and almost certainly derive from an earlier phase of composition (whatever its date, and whether primarily oral or literary). That being so, it looks as if the distinction between the usages of *Canu Aneirin* and *Canu Taliesin* and those of the rest may be a chronological and not merely an authorial one. This distinction is very clear and potentially very important. It implies a shift in terminology between an earlier phase and a later phase (although not, apparently, much shift in principle, either with respect to grades or to qualities of rulers).[14] It is the *words* that changed. For some reason, Welsh poets of the

---

[12] *Canu Aneirin,* 44a, 74, 98, 83; *Canu Taliesin,* 7. 1 (though this reference may be to successive rather than contemporary rulers).

[13] *Canu Llywarch Hen,* 6. 31. Cf. also use of *mechteyrn* for 'great ruler' in *Armes Prydein,* line 18; see above, n. 6, for reference to discussion of this term.

[14] Cf., at a later period, D. Jenkins on the increasing use of *arglwydd* for *brenin* in thirteenth-century law books, 'Kings, Lords, and Princes: The Nomenclature of Authority in Thirteenth-Century Wales', *Bulletin of the Board of Celtic Studies,* 26 (1974–6).

earlier phase chose different words to refer to rulers, of greater or lesser attributes; that earlier phase must lie somewhere between the sixth and tenth centuries inclusive, and probably seventh to ninth; it certainly lies before the eleventh century.

We can observe, then, that there was a clear change of terminology in the Latin sources: before the tenth century Latin writers preferred the single term *rex* for rulers, of various types and status and quality; in the mid- and later tenth century very few descriptive terms are used at all; while in the eleventh century and later we might well encounter the use of several very different terms. Although it is more difficult to assess precisely, there also seems to be a terminological shift in the vernacular sources, the words favoured in *Canu Aneirin* and *Canu Taliesin* either dropping out of the 'later' poetry or attracting greater emphasis and wider import. At the least this vernacular shift took place before the eleventh century, although it is quite impossible to give it precise chronological definition. Unfortunately, there is too little material to consider equivalence of Latin and vernacular terms in the early middle ages, and it is too inconsistent, although by the late thirteenth century there was clearly some stabilization; *Brut y Tywysogyon* consistently translates the Welsh Annals' *rex* with *brenin*, *princeps* with *tywysog*, and so on, just as there are consistent translations in the Latin texts of the Welsh laws.

QUALITIES OF RULERSHIP

There are a number of explicit statements in this material that some rulers were in some sense subject to others: the *mynawg*, Mynyddog of Eidyn, could attract rulers, leaders, and warriors from all over Britain to fight for him; the *gwledig* was associated with rule of the whole island of Britain, and even of heaven; Urien was chief, *arbenhic*, of the *teyrned* of *Canu Taliesin*; the independent Welsh kings of late ninth-century Wales could accept the *dominium* of the Saxon king Alfred.[15] Absolute power—total control—must have been unusual among Welsh kings, if not unknown, as it was highly unusual elsewhere in Europe at this period. This is scarcely surprising,

---

[15] *Canu Aneirin*, 68, 77; ibid. 17; *Canu Taliesin*, 11. 1; ibid. 3. 26; *Asser's Life of King Alfred*, ch. 80.

although it needs stating and emphasizing: sovereignty is not a concept which has much applicability in the early middle ages. One could nevertheless argue that ideas of sovereignty, or at least of an all-embracing power, were entertained; in ninth-century texts, both in the *Historia Brittonum* and on the Pillar of Eliseg, the word *monarchia* is used of imperial Roman power, with overtones of universal authority (though not of monarchy, 'single rule', in any strict sense). By the eleventh century, it could be suggested that Gruffudd ap Llywelyn held the 'monarchy' of the Britons; they cannot have supposed that a range of different political powers was concentrated in Gruffudd's hands alone, for this was patently obviously not so; but his territorial range was striking, and doubtless had an air of 'universality' about it.[16] It was presumably this wide range which influenced the Llandaff writer, rather than any perception of monarchy as we might understand it now. Throughout the early middle ages, fragmented power remained the norm.

Whether powers were full or partial, and held by greater or lesser rulers, they tended to be defined in relation to territory. So, the ruler ruled this or that *regio*, 'region'; boundaries were protected, defended, extended; territories are named, frequently, Argoed, Gwynedd, Dogfeiling, Gwent, and so on. It is perfectly clear from Latin and vernacular sources of all types and periods that the spatial extent of these territories was apparent to those using the terms: Gwent or Ceredigion were not abstract notions but pieces of land. Even in the work of Asser, writing in an English milieu (though himself Welsh), we find that the sense of territory predominates, and rulers are associated with rule of existing territorial units.[17] This strongly territorial framework to rule contrasts with English practice at the same period, for in England it was usual to define rule in relation to groups of people—king of the Hwicce, or the East Saxons, or the West Saxons, and so on. Of course, in Wales rulers did rule people as well as territory, but it is the idea of the territory that predominates; however, in certain special cases rule might be defined in terms of people: reference to a notional 'king of the Britons' is quite common. It is also worth

---

[16] *Historia Brittonum*, ch. 15, cf. ch. 19; *Book of Llan Dâv*, 266.

[17] *Canu Llywarch Hen*, 2. 1, 13. 9; *Annales Cambriae*, 547, 848; *Book of Llan Dâv*, nos. 234, 255; *Asser's Life of King Alfred*, ch. 80.

noting that in vernacular texts the word *gwlad* is used to express the notion 'sphere of rule', although a sphere which has a territorial dimension.[18] The *gwlad* was defendable, but was not necessarily the equivalent of a specific region: we hear of the *gwlad* that might be extended.[19] In Latin texts the equivalent of this term seems to be *regnum*, a word glossed by the cognate of *gwlad*, *flaith*, in Irish texts.[20] These *gwlad/regnum* words stand for 'rulerdom', 'kingdom' in the abstract sense, rather like German *königtum*; they refer primarily to the abstract idea of rule rather than to the actual territory ruled. *Gwlad* is not so much 'country', 'territory', 'political unit', a piece of ground and its people; but rather the changeable, expandable, contractable sphere of any ruler's power.[21]

By the tenth century, a region could be attached to other regions to form the real or supposed *gwlad/regnum* of a single ruler; hence, the compiler of the Harley collection of genealogies in the tenth century supposed that nine regions had been ruled by Cunedda.[22] Any ruler's *regnum/gwlad* might therefore be one *regio*, 'region', or several *regiones* or, presumably, part of a *regio*: the single inheritance of Powys was thus both a *regnum* and a *regio* in the inscription on the Pillar of Eliseg; but an eleventh- or twelfth-century editor of the Book of Llandaff saw Gwlad Forgan, Morgannwg, as composed of seven regions, and his king—the king of Morgannwg—encompassing them all in his sphere of rule.[23]

In most types of text and especially—and explicitly—in the vernacular, the most emphasized qualities of rulership at all periods are military: rulers are warriors and need to be

---

[18] *Canu Aneirin*, 94; *Canu Taliesin*, 1. 20, 23; ibid. 4. 15, 16; *Canu Llywarch Hen*, 3. 11, 8. 2; *Armes Prydein*, line 134.

[19] *Canu Taliesin*, 1.

[20] *Gulat* itself glosses *regia caeli*, 'the heavenly kingdom'; Stokes, *Trans. Phil. Soc.* (1860–1), 212. By the thirteenth century *Brut y Tywysogyon* uses *gwledychaud* for the *regnavit* of the Latin *Annales Cambriae*.

[21] See further below, p. 30.

[22] Bartrum, *Early Welsh Genealogical Tracts*, 13: Harleian MS 3859, no. 32.

[23] Ibid. 2; *Book of Llan Dâv*, 241. Since *regiones* are often classified as *cantrefi* in twelfth-century and later sources (cf. ibid., no. 247), it follows that a *gwlad* might be a *cantref*, or several; but neither *gwlad* nor *regio* has any necessary administrative import in pre-Conquest contexts. It requires more than the *existence* of a region to demonstrate that it had early administrative significance. See further below, p. 84 n. 10.

competent ones. Though the 'top' grades of ruler have qualities
beyond the military—wisdom, perfection, a wide reach—a
very high proportion of texts, whether Latin or vernacular,
refers to rulers in the midst of military activities and applauds
prowess above all else:

'Britain has kings', said Gildas '. . . they wage wars—civil and unjust.'

> For this is Urien,
> famous leader.
> He keeps the chiefs at bay
> and scythes them down. . . .
> the scourge of the men of Britain
>   in their battle lines,
> battle-sharpener at the station
>   of Ystrad Gwên.
> He did not spare nor field nor woods.

The grave of Môr the majestic, staunch chieftain (*unben*),
pillar in the swift-moving battle . . .

. . . Maredudd, king of Rheinwg, came to Glamorgan with a strong
force of enemies, that he might reign over it. Wherefore after arrival he
gave orders to gather loot and to drive off oxen to the camp for food.[24]
The ruler was himself a fighter, not merely a launcher of
armies or patron of champions. We should not lose sight of this
for it has a significant bearing on our understanding of lifestyle
and of administrative machinery too.

TERMS FOR POPULATION GROUPS

Although spheres of rule were much more usually defined in
terms of territory than of people, nevertheless group names did
exist and were used to distinguish and refer to groups of people.
We might take the case of 'Britons', to choose the lowest level
of definition. Britons, Saxons, Picts, and Cymry have their own
proper names (and occasionally, if rarely, group-defining words
like *clas*, 'community', are used in association with them).
These terms often correspond to distinct linguistic groups, just as
iaith, 'language', was itself used as a group-defining term: 'The

---

[24] *De excidio*, ch. 27 (trans. M. Winterbottom, Gildas, *The Ruin of Britain*
(Chichester, 1978)); *Canu Taliesin*, 2 (trans. M. Pennar); T. Jones, 'The Black
Book of Carmarthen "Stanzas of the Graves"', *Proc. British Academy*, 53
(1967), 123, no. 22; *Vita Cadoci*, ch. 41.

kings of every people (*ieith*) are all bound over to you . . .'.[25] However, there is more than one type of group name. Most commonly, territories gave a name to the people living on them, rather than the contrary (as occurred in many Germanic, Irish, and Roman contexts, where the East Saxons gave their name to Essex, the Connachta to Connaught, the Demetae to Dyfed, and so on). In Wales territories may well themselves have been named after individuals—Brycheiniog from Brychan, Meirionydd from Meirion, for instance—but the *group* term was derived from the existing territorial name and not vice versa. So, the region Gwent was associated with the people *Gwenhwys* ('Gwent', with a group-identifying suffix) or the *gwyr Guenti*, 'men of Gwent'; the region Brycheiniog with the *viri Broceniauc*, 'men of Brycheiniog'; or, as one inscribed stone implies, the region Elmet with the *Elmetiaci*, extrapolating from *Elmetiacos*, 'man of Elmet'.[26] Populations—groups of people—took their names from the territories they inhabited.

The word one might expect to find, *tud*—cognate of Irish *tuath*, 'people', the unit of rule in early medieval Ireland—is exceptionally rare.[27] In fact, the collective term most frequently used to refer to a population group in Latin sources is *gens*. This was sometimes a large group—like the four linguistic *gentes* of Britons, Saxons, Picts, and Scots that were seen to occupy the island of Britain; and it was sometimes quite explicitly used as an alternative to *regio*, 'region'; indeed, by the eleventh century it often meant little more than region, although as elsewhere in Europe it may well have been thought that the occupants of that region were 'a community of descent'. (So also, origin-tales devised eponymous ancestors,

---

[25] **Britons**: *Canu Aneirin*, 66b, 97; *Annales Cambriae*, 754; *Historia Brittonum*, cc. 23, 64, etc. **Picts**: *Annales Cambriae*, 775; *Historia Brittonum*, cc. 23, 30, 31, etc. **Cymry**: *Armes Prydein*, line 61. **Saxons**: ibid., line 133; *Annales Cambriae*, 757. **'Iaith'**: *Canu Taliesin*, 9. 15 (trans. Pennar).

[26] *Canu Taliesin*, 1. 10; cf. *Canu Aneirin*, 85; *Canu Llywarch Hen*, 3. 29; ibid. 2. 1; *Annales Cambriae*, 848; *ECMW*, no. 87.

[27] But see *Canu Taliesin*, 2. 9 and 8. 37: *tut*. Welsh law, however, retained the concept of the *alltud*, the 'foreigner'; cf. D. A. Binchy, *Celtic and Anglo-Saxon Kingship* (Oxford, 1970), 5, 7; in the law tracts, there was a residence qualification before the *alltud* could become a 'Welshman' (see Jenkins, *Law of Hywel*, 114–19; and T. M. Charles-Edwards, 'Some Celtic Kinship Terms', *Bull. Board Celt. Stud.*, 24 (1970–2), 116–17).

who gave their names to regions and who were thought to give
rise to lines of kings, like Ceredig of Ceredigion.)[28] If we look
for parallels to *gens* in vernacular sources, we find the word
llwyth for 'people', and occasionally *gwerin*.[29] It is more
important to note, however, that both collective terms were
infrequently used; proper names were more usual. When the
early medieval Welsh talked about people, they said 'the men
of Gwent' or the 'Gwynedd people', not this or that 'tribe'.

Naming practice therefore suggests that group identity was
conceived either very broadly, essentially linguistically, or as
dependent on residence in a named territory. Only in particular
circumstances might a group coincide with a *gwlad*. This
characteristically territorial approach to social identity is
sometimes openly expressed, and becomes very explicit in the
eleventh century. The Annals talk of the desertion of the
'fatherland' (*patria*) and late in the century we have one
individual who expressed his identification with the territory
where he lived: Ieuan ap Sulien, of the episcopal family of St
David's, of Llanbadarn origin, in a well-written poem elabor-
ated on his commitment to his country, Ceredigion, and
detailed its physical characteristics with love and respect. Born
of the *gens* of the Britons, he says, Ceredigion was his *patria*,

---

[28] *Historia Brittonum*, ch. 7; *De excidio*, ch. 21 (of *all* the Britons); Ieuan's
poem on Sulien (Lapidge, 'Welsh-Latin Poetry', *Studia Celtica*, 8–9 (1973–4),
82), lines 51, 54 (of Britons, and of his father); *Historia Brittonum*, cc. 24
('duces Romanicae gentis'), 30 ('gentes barbarorum'), 43 ('reges nostrae
gentis'); *Vita Cadoci*, ch. 25: 'si minus seruauerit gentem Gunliuensem . . .
Orauit igitur sanctus Cadocus ad Dominum, ut daret ei regem, qui pro eo suam
gentem regeret . . . Patrocinare meam patriam atque hereditatem Gundliauc',
cf. ch. 23, 'suos tironos ad regionem Guunliauc direxit'. However, *boned*,
'family', glosses *gens* in the tenth-century MS, Oxford Bodleian 572, Stokes,
Trans. Phil. Soc. (1860–1), 219; cf. *genealogia* as an alternative to *prouincia* in
the Colloquy in the same manuscript, *Early Scholastic Colloquies*, ed.
Stevenson, 1. 9, sect. 24: 'Quo tempore peruenisti ad istam prouinciam, uel
patriam, uel ad istam genealogiam, uel ad istam regionem'. Cf. S. Reynolds,
'Medieval *Origines Gentium* and the Community of the Realm', *History*, 68
(1983), 377–80, where she cites a mass of evidence that in western Europe in
the tenth to thirteenth centuries it was believed that 'peoples' ought to
coincide with political units; see also her *Kingdoms and Communities*, 254–6.
For origin tales, see for example *Historia Brittonum*, cc. 48, 49; Bartrum, *Early
Welsh Genealogical Tracts*, 13: Harleian MS 3859, no. 32.

[29] *Armes Prydein*, line 128; D. Jenkins and M. E. Owen, 'The Welsh
Marginalia in the Lichfield Gospels, Pt. 1', *Cambridge Medieval Celtic
Studies*, 5 (1983), 51. Cf. *gwerin* and its 'chief', 'elder', *Canu Taliesin*, 6. 23, and
guerin glossing *factio*, 'multitude', Stokes, *Trans. Phil. Soc.* (1860–1), 212.

its bounds being clearly marked by the sea, rivers and mountains:

That the land of Ceredig is certainly my homeland, I confess openly to all . . . This (land) exhibits the form of a table with four sides. For a lofty mountain rises at the source of the sun, advantageous (in providing) much pasture for flocks. An immense river irrigates the right-hand side (of the country); and then the wide sea washes the western side. But a mighty river divides the region of the north. Thus by the sea, together with the mountain and the two rivers, this fertile region is discerned on all sides.[30]

POWER OVER PEOPLE

People might identify more closely with their homelands than their rulers but most of them were nevertheless ruled by someone, whether local or distant. Someone, or several people, had power over them. Power over people seems to have been viewed in different ways—principally as patronage, as ownership, and as a vague yet different 'rulership', and therefore appropriate to clients, the unfree, and the subject respectively. All are familiar approaches in other European cultures of the same, and different, periods. One must also suppose the existence of another quality of power: the power of the head of a household over its members other than clients, a power which at the least affected women and minors, and which would limit the freedom of the individual to change his or her state (into marriage or religion, for example) and to perform legal actions (be sureties, give evidence in dispute proceedings, make contracts). There is no direct pre-twelfth-century Welsh evidence of this latter quality of power, but it is likely to have existed in some form since it is evident in later Welsh legal material, as also in earlier Irish and Breton texts.[31]

It is in fact easiest to discuss these powers from the point of

---

[30] *Annales Cambriae*, 1049; Ieuan's poem on Sulien (Lapidge, 'Welsh-Latin Poetry', *Studia Celtica*, 8–9 (1973–4), 82–4), lines 54–72; though cf. also 'Canu Heledd', *Canu Llywarch Hen*, 11. Huw Pryce points out that in the twelfth century Llywelyn Fardd's *Canu i Gadfan* combines praise of a saint with praise of the locality of Meirionydd, *Hen Gerddi Crefyddol*, ed. H. Lewis (Cardiff, 1931), no. 35, especially lines 47–8, 95–6.

[31] *Die irische Kanonensammlung*, ed. F. W. H. Wasserschleben (2nd edn.; Leipzig, 1885), 34. 3; see also W. Davies, 'Celtic Women in the Early Middle Ages', in *Images of Women in Antiquity*, ed. A. Cameron and A. Kuhrt (London, 1983), 148–9. Huw Pryce has argued persuasively that this eighth-century Irish

view of the subject person—that is as clientship, as the dependence of menials, and as 'being a subject'.

Clientship

Clientship is very familiar. Although vernacular texts are the most obvious source, Latin texts from all periods also show clientship in operation, although doing so in a more matter of fact way than the vernacular.[32] In this material, patronage was inevitably an attribute of rulership: if you had clients you were a ruler, since at least you ruled *them*. In practice what this relationship meant was that the ruler provided material support (chattels, stock, even occasionally lands and weapons) for his following, the clients; generosity was expected of him; the clients had a sense of commitment to, even love for, the patron and themselves supported him (usually by fighting, but sometimes in other ways like writing poems). It was a relationship of mutual support, and contact between the parties was close:

The lord in the bloodshed, hastening on the border, the grey-haired one who sustained us, on his front-line skittish steed, in rugged shape . . .

or

> There is a fine fortress, where a multitude
> Makes loud revelry, and so do the singing birds.
> Joyous were its songs at the Calends
> About a generous lord, bold, and brave.
> Before his passing into the oaken church,
> He gave me mead and wine out of a crystal bowl.
>
> There is a fine fortress on the promontory,
> Graciously each one there receives his share . . .
> My custom it was on New Year's Eve
> To sleep beside my prince, the glorious in battle,
> And wear a purple mantle, and enjoy (every) luxury,
> So that I have become the tongue of Britain's bards.[33]

text clearly influenced later Welsh law texts, and must have been borrowed in Wales in the pre-Conquest period, 'Early Irish Canons and Medieval Welsh Law', *Peritia*, 5 (1986).

[32] *De excidio*, ch. 27; *Historia Brittonum*, cc. 43, 46; *Book of Llan Dâv*, nos. 218, 225, 237b, 249b, 257, 261, 264a, 267, 271, 272; *Vita Cadoci*, cc. 6, 8, 16, 19, 23, 26 (the saint as the 'fidelis cliens' of God).

[33] *Canu Aneirin*, 42 (trans. Jackson). 'Etmic Dinbych', lines 27–34, 37–40,

Clients were therefore literally the following of a ruler, their patron, and at least temporarily members of his household.[34] There is no need to suppose that patron/client relationships were always or even normally permanent, nor that clients were in year-round residence; we should see the arrangements as short-term and flexible in a world of fluid and changing relationships. Perhaps surprisingly, clients might themselves be rulers and accordingly might have their own clients; so, some of the *teyrned* of *Canu Aneirin* were clients of the great *mynawg*, Mynyddog, 'lord of hosts'.[35] This fact emphasizes the absence of sovereignty, and the wide distribution of political power, as indicated above.

Although the patron inevitably had the power over his clients that came with support, although he led and directed them, there is nothing in this material which suggests that he had total power over them; there is no emphasis on binding or pledging of client to supporter. The relationship does not look the same as the institution of vassalage as it developed in tenth-, eleventh-, and twelfth-century Europe: in Wales it was not lifelong; it did not become territorialized; it did not have so many associated rules and institutions (like wardship and marriage, for instance); it had fewer consequences and far fewer repercussions.[36] These characteristics are as applicable to Welsh material of the tenth and eleventh centuries as to that

---

in I. Williams, *The Beginnings of Welsh Poetry*, ed. and trans. R. Bromwich (Cardiff, 1972), 164–5. Cf. *Canu Aneirin*, 85; *Canu Taliesin*, 1, 4, 5; *Canu Llywarch Hen*, 3.

[34] *Coscoruaur* (*gosgordd fawr*), 'retinue', glosses *familia magna*, 'household', in Middle Welsh, and in Old Cornish, and *casgoord* glosses *satilites*, 'cronies', 'accomplices', in Old Welsh; *dau(u)*, 'following', eventually 'son-in-law', glosses *cliens* in Old Breton and Old Welsh, but *gener* in Old Cornish; see Stokes, *Trans. Phil. Soc.* (1860–1), 234, 249, and also *Trioedd Ynys Prydein*, ed. R. Bromwich (Cardiff, 1961), 65–6. The semantic range here emphasizes the nearness of the following, the physical closeness of clientship: words for family or its members are used to denote members of the retinue too; all are members of the household.

[35] *Canu Aneirin*, 66a, 67a. Cf. nobles (i.e. persons with *flaith*, 'political power') as clients in early Ireland, *Críth Gablach*, ed. D. A. Binchy (Dublin, 1941), sect. 27. See further below, n. 49.

[36] For a useful summary of material and problems see J.-P. Poly and E. Bournazel, *La Mutation féodale* (Paris, 1980). NB *Canu Aneirin*, 35, refers to 'eillt Mynyddog' of a warrior; the meaning of *eillt* here is surely 'nourished', or even 'friend', rather than 'pledged'; cf. L. Fleuriot, *Dictionnaire des gloses en vieux bretonne* (Paris, 1964), 59, s.v. *alt*.

of the sixth and seventh; although starting from comparable beginnings, Welsh clientship did not share the same passage of development as continental vassalage. Nor do clients appear to have been treated like ordinary members of the household, despite the clients' membership of a large one: to judge by poetry and anecdotes, they retained freedom of action, presumably some legal capacity, and clearly some independent military power.[37] Clientship, then, was largely to do with the patterns of mutual support among a military aristocracy.

Dependence of menials

The type of power over people that we would describe as 'ownership' meant dependence for those in power, a state which might more usefully be called 'servitude' but for the many and varied overtones. This is again familiar. To have low-status dependants, without military capacity, supported on the landed property of the ruler, was as much an attribute of rulership as was patronage. In practice it must have meant control of the product of the dependants' labour and hence of their powers of movement: they could not go away nor terminate the relationship; like most members of a household, they could not make contracts nor be sureties; they had no powers of negotiation, and hence the tag of 'perpetual servitude' that we find in the charters and the *Vitae*. They were therefore more constrained than ordinary members of a household. However, I do not think that this relationship involved labour service—the badge of serfdom in central and late medieval Europe—because there are neither direct nor implicit indications of it in early medieval Wales. The lack of any such indication is very striking.

The existence of menials in Wales is clearly evidenced in the Latin sources from the eighth century onwards.[38] Comparable suggestions are very rare in the vernacular sources

[37] This is evidenced at all periods in Latin texts, early *and* late; see above, n. 32, for references; cf. Davies, *Conquest, Coexistence, and Change*, 66–70.

[38] *Book of Llan Dâv*, nos. 127a, 185, 207, 236; Stevenson (ed.), *Early Scholastic Colloquies*, 1. 11, sect. 27: 'Serui, subiecti estote, et ite propere ad opus uestrum . . . Et dicit unus de seruis, uel captiuis'; *Vita Cadoci*, cc. 7, 33, 34; *Historia Brittonum*, cc. 35, 50.

(largely because their primary concern is with military society itself), although bondage words, like *caeth* and *eillt*, do sometimes occur in contexts which lack detail of the relationships implied.[39] However, it is possible to argue that the existence and early appearances of the word *gwas*, 'servant', must imply vernacular reference to a stratum of bound dependants in Brittonic (and continental Celtic) societies from a very early, pre-eighth-century, date. The Celtic word *gwas*, 'servant', 'boy', was the word borrowed into Latin to give *vassus*, 'vassal' and other dependants, in continental Europe. The Brittonic term occurs in Old Breton glosses with the clear meaning of 'bound', 'pledged': 'di im damguas' glosses 'si quis se iuramento constrixerit' ('if anyone be bound . . .'), for example, and 'guos' glosses *stipulationes* ('guarantees', 'pledges'); many of the earliest uses of the Latin borrowing are domestic and menial rather than relating to vassalage, suggesting that the term was borrowed because of its overtones of commitment and subjection.[40] Moreover, since *gwas* was *not* used in Wales to gloss *cliens*, 'military client', it looks as if it was a term used to refer to (domestic) menials, bound to their masters, at the time of the glossing.[41] It is interesting to note that the word also occurs on an inscribed stone of early date (probably of the fifth or sixth century), from Llantrisant in Anglesey; a bishop is there described as *vasso Paulini*, a follower, an adherent, of St Paulinus. The term seems to have been adopted by clerics to express their commitment to religion, the pledging of their lives and bodies to God and his saints; *vasso Paulini*, *gwas Diu*, *guos Cadog* thereby occur in Brittonic texts, describing people committed to St Paulinus,

---

[39] *Canu Taliesin*, 1. 25; *Armes Prydein*, line 34; 'Etmic Dinbych', line 24, in Williams, *Beginnings*, ed. Bromwich: *kaeth* (subject and of the lowest status).

[40] Fleuriot, *Dictionnaire*, 141, 183, 199; cf. J. F. Niermeyer, *Mediae Latinitatis Lexicon Minus* (Leiden, 1976), 1063–5; Poly/Bournazel, *Mutation féodale*, 106–10.

[41] Stokes, *Trans. Phil. Soc.* (1860–1), 234; cf. Fleuriot, *Dictionnaire*, 130. The essential difference in the approach to the menial (*gwas*) and the client (*dauu*) seems to be that menials were 'pledged', bound to *future* performance, but clients were not; the clients were companions, whose commitment was to do with the immediate, the short-term, rather than to the future. When client relationships became territorialized, as they did in continental Europe and England, they acquired a future dimension too.

God, and St Cadog.[42] The range of use of this word is therefore for non-military dependants, rather than warriors with some capacity for independent action. Its use therefore implies the existence—as a norm—of a stratum of bound dependants at an early post-Roman date.

Now it is also clear that slavery existed in early Wales, that is slavery in the sense of complete ownership of one individual by another; one text written into the margins of the Lichfield Gospels, of ninth-century date, records the manumission of a slave and his offspring who bought his own freedom for 4 lb. and 8 oz. (of silver). Elsewhere in the south, at a surprisingly late date, there are recorded grants of individual dependants to churches in 'perpetual servitude': the latest recorded gift of people (without any reference to lands they might work) took place round about 980 and was made to the abbot of Llancarfan in the Vale of Glamorgan; in the mid-tenth century, not far away at St Arvans on the River Wye, perpetual servitude was considered an appropriate penalty in a judgment following a case of breach of sanctuary and the killing of a homicidal deacon; this can only mean penal slavery.[43] We do not know that there was any qualitative difference between slavery and the sort of menial dependence already discussed: there may well have been varieties of dependence and therefore gradations of 'status' within the fully dependent strata; after all, we know of *heredes* (tied tenants) who directed their own labour at least up to the ninth century, people who (though tied) may have had a greater element of self-determination in their lives than the penal or hereditary slaves. Whether or not there *were* such gradations, we are unlikely to discover; but that there was a fundamental distinction between free and unfree is evident and important. When Thomas Charles-Edwards, in an earlier Oxford O'Donnell lecture, argued that there was an essential difference between freedom and unfreedom in early Welsh society, he argued this for quite different reasons; but he made a significant point and the argument makes sense on a range of different counts.[44]

---

[42] *ECMW*, no. 33; see further Fleuriot, *Dictionnaire*, 199.
[43] *Book of Llan Dâv*, p. xlvi; ibid., no. 243, cf. nos. 127a, 185, 218.
[44] In Oxford in 1979.

'Being a subject'

The third category of power over people, for which it is difficult to find a word other than 'rulership', and its converse, 'being a subject', are more difficult to demonstrate since the relationship between ruler and subject is often implicit, but its nature unspecified. Some texts (the *Historia Brittonum*, the *Vita Cadoci*, some vernacular poems, for example) explicitly say that entire populations of given regions were deemed 'subject' to rulers, whether or not they were clients or dependants. So, the 'whole region' of Powys was ruled by the Cadelling; Maelgwn ruled over the 'whole of Britain'; a king had to be found to rule the region of Gwynllŵg.[45] Rulers ruled, controlled, governed (usually *regere* in Latin) the territory, and therefore such people as lived on it. The rule of a territory and its population may not have meant very much in practice. Those texts that are explicit about rulership of this type only hint at its implications: clearly the ruler was expected to protect the territory and its people from attack, and prevent depletion of their resources; almost as clearly—in the later Latin texts especially—he was associated with the possibility of tax-taking: phrases evoking the rule of the Romans in the *Historia Brittonum* talk of the *census*-taking that that rule implied; the eleventh-century Life of Cadog's image of Maelgwn, as ruler of all Britain, was that he came, terrifyingly, to collect his *census*, while the same Life presented King Meurig of Gwynllŵg as charged to keep taxes low in *his* kingdom. Beyond this there is little, except a general sense of expectation of obedience to orders.[46]

Of course, there was no necessary identity of interest between a population and the man that ruled its territory; he was not its representative and might well have different interests. It is therefore not surprising to find that there are occasions in the ninth, tenth, and eleventh centuries when action was taken by the men of a region—of Brycheiniog, of

---

[45] *Historia Brittonum*, ch. 35, cf. ch. 30; *Vita Cadoci*, cc. 23, 25; cf. *Canu Taliesin*, 1. 25.

[46] *Canu Taliesin*, 1. 23, 2. 9–10, and 4. 15–16; *Historia Brittonum*, cc. 19, 20, 28, 30; *Vita Cadoci*, cc. 23, 25; *Historia Brittonum*, ch. 33. Later, the law tracts ascribe enactments to Bleddyn ap Cynfyn (*Llyfr Iorwerth*, ed. A. R. Wiliam (Cardiff, 1960), sect. 82, 115).

Ystrad Tywi—certainly without their ruler and sometimes in direct opposition to him. In the South-East, at least, the Llandaff charters also make it clear that there were groups of local men in the eighth and ninth centuries who saw to the transaction of local business and regulation of local relationships in areas of some thirty miles radius—regardless of the interests and activities of their rulers.[47]

WORDS, RULE, AND PEOPLE

If we consider the ideas about rule in early Wales that are communicated by words themselves and the contexts of their use, we might summarize as follows: there were plenty of words for ruler used in early Wales, and plenty of rulers indicated, although Latin and vernacular texts did so in different ways and the vernacular terminology was more extensive than the Latin. Rulers might be of different quality: the relationship between a patron and his clients was seen as one between ruler and ruled, as also that between a landlord and his dependants, and that between another man and his 'subjects'. War leaders, landlords, and those with subjects were all perceived as rulers, although rulers of varying status. In other words: all rulers were landlords; some rulers were merely landlords; some landlords had clients; and some of the landlords who had clients also had control of territories and of associated populations who were neither clients nor dependants (see Fig. 1). Those that were merely landlords, or were landlords with clients, had lesser status and were themselves usually subject to the rule of a ruler of higher status. They must have included the *optimates* and *viri* who sometimes took independent military action against or in spite of their local kings, as also the abbots and bishops who had a considerable number of dependants and sometimes wide-

---

[47] See W. Davies, *An Early Welsh Microcosm* (London, 1978), 108–10; cf. *Brut y Tywysogyon, RBH Version*, 1115, where the 'elders' (*henafyeit*) of Llŷn worked with the bishops against Gruffudd ap Cynan. NB *gwerin*, 'people', 'host', and its chief (literally 'elder', *einewyd*) in *Canu Taliesin*, 6. 23—there could just be some identity of interest in mind here. My comments in this paragraph are quite contrary to those of Susan Reynolds, who sees 'kingdoms as communities' in most of western Europe in the period 900–1300, *Kingdoms and Communities*, 262–302.

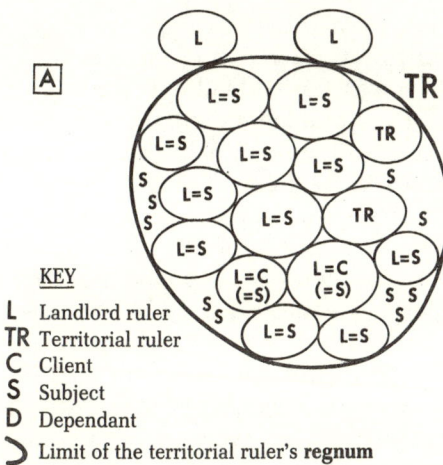

KEY

L Landlord ruler
TR Territorial ruler
C Client
S Subject
D Dependant
⊃ Limit of the territorial ruler's **regnum**

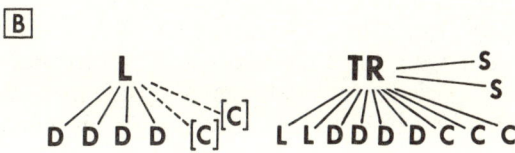

FIG.1 Diagram to illustrate ruler relationships

ranging properties.[48] All, however, were associated with powers of direction backed by actual or potential military force—most rulers were themselves warriors—and all were necessarily landlords; we are dealing with a landed warrior aristocracy with considerable powers of control over its immediate dependants. We should not forget that this was an aristocracy whose powers of rule, whether limited or wide, were generally accepted. They all had an acknowledged political power—that is the ability to direct, command, constrain; limitations on their power do not appear to have rested in any constitutional or popular constraints; if there

[48] This does not have to mean that there were no free peasant cultivators, nor that everyone was ruled.

were any limitations, they rested in the power of contemporaries to limit the territorial reach of one another.

In practice the powers of a landlord were to do with monopolizing production and labour and maximizing income, together with day-to-day direction (by himself or an agent): he gave orders. Landlords with clients had this, but also had an enhanced managerial role—a wider range of orders to give, a wider range of people to direct, a need to provide immediate (personal) leadership. Landlords with clients *and* subjects had all this but also perhaps some capacity to generate income (take tax) from those who were *not* their own dependants; and a capacity to give orders similarly. These are not essentially different powers from those of rulers of lower status but their exercise is different in that the types of people affected are more, the number greater, the range wider—Mynyddog 'of wide reach', as the poets say. These rulers clearly expected to rule people who had their own clients and menial dependants. It is *this* sphere of rule that is *gwlad* and *regnum*, these rulers who were the 'kings' of the Latin texts.

Most rulers were therefore necessarily subject to some other ruler, either as clients or as elements of the population subject to the wider territorial control, fiscal demands, and ordinance-making attempts of another. This manifestation of political power—its fragmentation and distribution amongst several parties—though differently expressed, is at least comparable to some early Irish concepts (as also, though differently organized, to tenth- and eleventh-century west Frankish practice).[49]

However, it needs more than consideration of words and ideas to perceive the operation of power in early medieval Wales; bearing in mind the terminological shift which, in Latin texts at least, can be tied down to the period c.950–1020, we need to think of practice, that is of actions as well as of

---

[49] *Críth Gablach*, ed. Binchy, sect. 23; see W. Davies, 'Clerics as Rulers', in *Latin and the Vernacular Languages in Early Medieval Britain*, ed. N. Brooks (Leicester, 1982), 90. In Ireland the *rí*, 'king', as well as others (*flaithemhain*), had political authority (*flaith*); a *rí* was *flaithem* as well as *rí*. What made the king the king (*rí* more than *flaithem*) was his additional functions, but he was perceived as sharing the same range of political powers as the nobility. For some detailed discussion of the concepts here, see B. K. Lambkin, 'The Structure of Sacred and Secular Lordship in the Poems of Blathmac', MA thesis (The Queen's University, Belfast, 1985).

thoughts; and we need a diachronic dimension as well as the bundle of synchronic dimensions which the texts as texts represent. There seems—on the evidence of words alone—to have been some hiatus in perceptions of rulers, if not rulership, in the late tenth and eleventh centuries; can we relate this to actions?

3. Practice

Looking at words used in early medieval Welsh texts, and words alone, suggests some shift in perceptions of rulership in the tenth and early eleventh centuries. Looking at words also suggests that rulership had an essentially military quality and that there was a strong territorial basis to the definition of a rulerdom, as also to the formulation of group identity. However, it is as important to consider actions as ideas—what people did as much as ways of looking at things—if we want to investigate the *exercise* of power within early medieval Wales. It is a concern with actual practice, then, which is the subject of this chapter. I shall begin by making a quick survey of political history until the late eleventh century, as conventionally told;[1] then, after some consideration of the pre-ninth-century background, I shall go on to probe political relationships between Welsh rulers in the ninth- to eleventh-century period. For the moment, interest is specifically in Welshmen's relationships with, and reactions to, each other; of course they interacted with others too, English and Scandinavians especially, but I shall delay consideration of this other interaction until the next chapters.

A POLITICAL SURVEY

From at least the early sixth century Welsh politics were dominated by kings (the *reges* of the Latin texts and 'territorial rulers' of the last chapter), who—in the earlier centuries—were clearly associated with territorial kingdoms.[2] These early kingdoms of Wales included Gwynedd, Dyfed, Powys, Brycheiniog, and Glywysing, in north-west, south-west, north-east, centre east and south-east respectively, and each had a long life of several—sometimes many—centuries (see Fig. 2). Now the term Gwynedd denoted a recognizable area of land as well as a

---

[1] I gave a full political survey in Davies, *Wales*, 85–120; I would not draw the main lines of it any differently now.

[2] See ibid. 90–102.

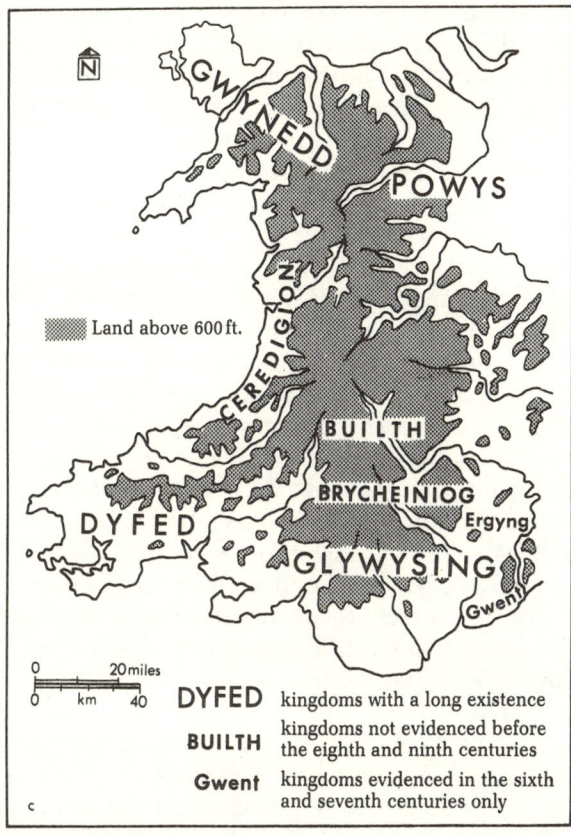

Land above 600 ft.

DYFED kingdoms with a long existence

BUILTH kingdoms not evidenced before the eighth and ninth centuries

Gwent kingdoms evidenced in the sixth and seventh centuries only

FIG.2 Early kingdoms of Wales (after Davies, *Wales*, Fig. 32, by permission of Leicester University Press)

kingdom, as did the other terms. There were also regions that had a recognized identity which did not coincide with any *political* unit: Gwent and Ceredigion, for example, were always well-known regions but were often regions within larger kingdoms. Some clearly identifiable regions, then, were also independent kingdoms; others were not. Some were *gwledydd*; others were not.

While some of the newly established kings may well have been the heirs of the late Roman provincial administrative system, and may have contrived over a couple of centuries to operate increasingly devolved late Roman institutions, it is clear that the fifth and sixth centuries witnessed some level of political dislocation. Irish raids provoked the refortification of late Roman forts at least at Caernarfon and Cardiff, while the tendency to reoccupy Iron-Age hillforts in this period suggests some widely felt need for defence or at least some politically aggressive initiatives: forts like Degannwy and Dinas Emrys have political associations in the surviving early medieval literature; others like Dinas Powys and Dinorben may have had so too, though unnoted. It is therefore likely that there was some military activity at this time, although—with very minimal sources—we cannot even guess at the scale of it nor the proportion of the population affected. The likelihood is that it was largely a matter for the aristocracy, that is for those creating and contending for the kingships. We know, at least, that the kings of Gwynedd were involved in very wide-ranging raiding by the seventh century, eastwards into midland and even northern Britain. Powys kings may well have raided the English midlands too in the early seventh century, although by the end of that century they seem to have suffered from the successes of the English kings, who ultimately confined Powys territory to a rather limited area in eastern Wales.

Kingly activities in the South-East seem to have been more confined, and we do not hear of comparable long-range raiding. However, we do have some indication of the politics of the region itself: the several tiny kingdoms of the sixth and early seventh centuries were absorbed into a single kingdom of Glywysing by the early eighth century, as the newly established dynasty of Meurig ap Tewdrig worked its way from the Wye mouth northwards into Ergyng and westwards into the vale of Glamorgan. By the mid-eighth century King Ithel of Glywysing seemed poised to build upon this amalgamation of smaller units and develop a workable administrative system, a new system that was appropriate for time and place rather than a hangover of archaic practices.[3]

Most people believe that Offa's Dyke was constructed near the line of the present English/Welsh border in the late eighth century, thus defining a boundary between English and Welsh, and marking the isolation of the Welsh from their eastern

---

[3] See Davies, *Microcosm*, 65–95.

British one-time fellows and allies (see Fig. 7). Thereafter there were changes in the existing Welsh political structures: in the early ninth century came dynastic change in Dyfed and Gwynedd and much English activity in Powys; as a consequence, a weakened Powys seems to have been absorbed by the kings of Gwynedd into the larger and more powerful kingdom; a little later Ceredigion was similarly absorbed. To what extent this 'absorption' involved any real political control is arguable; it certainly is not demonstrable.[4] However, what *is* clear is that Powys and Ceredigion lost any separate *political* identity that they had earlier had. The ninth century, then, is a period marked more than anything else by the ambition of the kingdom of Gwynedd; this is especially notable under King Rhodri Mawr, 'Rhodri the Great' (d. 878), although his son Anarawd raided extensively in the south in the later ninth century, such that the kings of the south sought 'protection' from the West Saxon king Alfred.

Meanwhile Viking raids on the coasts of Wales had begun in the mid-ninth century and continued intermittently for the next sixty years or so; these raids do not appear to have engendered any large-scale political disruption. The South-East, still ruled by branches of the main Glywysing dynasty of kings, remained in many respects separate from the rest of Wales, although it too suffered from Anarawd's attacks.

Early in the tenth century one of the Gwynedd dynasty married into the royal line of Dyfed, perhaps following his father's political conquest of part of the area, and for a short period in the 940s both Dyfed and Gwynedd were notionally ruled by that man—Hywel, commonly known as Hywel Dda, 'Hywel the Good'. In a sense a high proportion of the land of Wales was then ruled by a single ruler, a circumstance which might superficially suggest some movement towards the establishment of a single kingdom of Wales, and which has given Hywel a central position in the historiography of early Welsh political development. However, the period was short (at most

---

[4] I agree with David Dumville's observation that 'Neither annexation [of Powys and Ceredigion] is stated explicitly in the annalistic texts . . . We merely deduce from the silence of Asser and all later sources that Powys fell under Venedotian control before c. 890', 'The "Six" Sons of Rhodri Mawr: A Problem in Asser's *Life of King Alfred*', *Cambridge Medieval Celtic Studies*, 4 (1982), 15. Much later, in the later eleventh century, Powys re-emerged as a political entity.

eight years) and both kingdoms retained their separate identities. Hywel's horizons were certainly wider than this and he—like several other Welsh rulers—entered into a relationship with the increasingly powerful English monarchy; as a result, these Welsh kings intermittently attended the royal court in England.[5]

As Hywel died, Scandinavian attacks were beginning again, and continued through the second half of the tenth century and into the eleventh. Throughout this period the kingdoms of Gwynedd, Dyfed, and Glywysing—the last now known as Morgannwg—continued to exist, Dyfed and Gwynedd each drawing kings from the same dynasty and the South-East remaining apart from that dynasty's interest. Brycheiniog disappears from the record as a separate and distinct political unit after the late tenth century.[6] For all the continuities, the most striking political development of the tenth century is the fact that in all areas, south as well as north, there was dynastic instability. From about 950 several new families established themselves contemporaneously as rulers in the South-East, thereby destroying the long established cohesion of the single kingdom of Glywysing/Morgannwg. The same is true of the South-West in the early eleventh century, as a series of short-lived intruders, like the Irishman Rhain, of no very certain pedigree, established themselves as kings in Dyfed.

In the second quarter of the eleventh century a member of one of the intrusive dynasties of the South-East—Rhydderch ab Iestyn—was considered by some to rule 'all Wales'. His son, Gruffudd ap Rhydderch, moved into the South-West and started to range over the whole of southern Wales, physically moving throughout the area and engaging in military conflict with those who opposed him. (In fact the family may well ultimately have been of south-west origin.) By the 1040s he was engaged with another Gruffudd (ap Llywelyn), and their conflict in the period 1045–55 dominates the political record. Gruffudd ap Llywelyn was the son of another aristocratic adventurer who had bid for power in the south, but Gruffudd himself apparently first established himself in the north (by 1039). Both Gruffudds also increasingly came into contact with English and Normans on

---

[5] See below, p. 74.

[6] In the mid-tenth century Hywel seems to have been staying in Brycheiniog; *Book of Llan Dâv*, no. 218.

the borders of Wales. Eventually, in 1055, Gruffudd ap Llywelyn killed Gruffudd ap Rhydderch and thereafter notionally ruled all Wales (including the South-East) until he himself was killed by his own men in 1063, following English campaigns. Earl Harold then took hostages for King Edward of England, who appointed Bleddyn and Rhiwallon, Gruffudd's half-brothers, to Welsh rulerships. Shortly afterwards the Norman Conquest of England began and Wales was soon enmeshed in the new political situation. In fact, Welsh leaders had already been tangling with the Normans on the borders since the 1050s; in the new situation the border conflict was quickly directed to Wales itself and in the late 1060s and early 1070s new Norman lords rode into Wales from Hereford, Chester, and Shrewsbury.[7]

THE PRE-NINTH-CENTURY BACKGROUND

Although there is good reason to think that political structures in Wales were undergoing considerable change in and from the ninth century, some aspects of the pre-ninth-century development are important for the long term. It is absolutely clear that in Wales, as in wider Britain, political units (i.e.'territorial' or 'top' rulerships) were established some time after Roman government of Britain ended early in the fifth century. This must mean that the political situation of Wales changed dramatically: Wales was no longer a small part of a large empire, of considerable administrative sophistication, but a mosaic of very small (independent) political units. We know virtually nothing about the circumstances of the establishment of these units but we do know that several existed by the early sixth century and that some were in at least their second generation of rulers by then. In other words, they were fifth-century creations. Although the process of this change is sketchy, the fact of it is very important both for that period and for the future. We also know little of their characteristics but these units were relatively

[7] Ibid., no. 253 and p. 252; cf. *Annales Cambriae*, 1033: when Rhydderch was killed (by the *Irish*), Iago [i.e. of Gwynedd] and the sons of Edwin [i.e. of Dyfed] held his *regio*. For the Gruffudds, and the Normans, see Davies, *Conquest, Coexistence, and Change*, 25–31; C. P. Lewis, 'English and Norman Government and Lordship in the Welsh Borders, 1039–87', D.Phil. thesis (University of Oxford, 1985), especially 298, 323, 328. The issues are, of course, much more complicated than I present here.

small (county size or even smaller) and they were defined with
reference to territory rather than to population groups; that is,
in accordance with the usual early medieval Welsh practice,
they are referred to as the kingdom of such and such a place not
the kingdom of such and such a people. Already in the sixth
century the power to rule was transmitted dynastically: any
given kingship was dominated by a particular family and power
was handed on through that family from generation to generation. This was as true of Romanized as of un-Romanized
Wales, just as it was true of north and south-west Britain, and
quite possibly east and midland Britain too.[8] It is particularly
interesting to note that dynastic interests are established, and
accepted in the surviving literature, at such an early date.

Secondly, whereas in Britain as a whole these early British
kingdoms tended to disappear in the course of the seventh
century, as they were replaced by newly established English
kings, in western Britain the early kingdoms continued; hence
Dumnonia and Strathclyde, as well as the Welsh kingdoms,
have a history of several centuries. But in Wales, as time passed
there were changes to the framework apparent in the sixth
century. By the eighth century there seem to be different trends
in different parts of Wales: in the South-East there was a
reduction in the number of political units, because some were
absorbed by the kingdom of Glywysing, over several generations;
but elsewhere, more units are evidenced. This must mean either
that new kingdoms were being established outside the South-
East in the eighth century; or that there is simply more evidence
available for those parts in the eighth century. Whichever is the
truth, there clearly was no *reduction* in the number of northern
and western kingdoms at that time; in other words, seventh-/
eighth-century development there was different from that of the
South-East, for there is nothing which suggests political con-
solidation. Notwithstanding the fact that south-eastern evidence is much more detailed and much more easily localizable,
one can see why south-eastern trends, with the romanized

---

[8] See Davies, *Wales*, 122–3; *Historia Brittonum*, ch. 37, assumes that there
was a British king ruling in Kent when Hengest arrived there in the fifth century;
cf. James Campbell's comments on the British royal antecedents of the Anglian
dynasty at Yeavering in Northumberland, Campbell and others, *The Anglo-
Saxons* (Oxford, 1982), 57.

background and largely good agricultural terrain of the area, should indeed have been different from those of the rest of the country.

Thirdly, the Irish. The evidence for Irish settlement in Wales is not straightforward but is, overall, positive. The key elements of this evidence are place-names indicating the presence of Irish speakers and memorial stones inscribed with the Irish alphabet (ogham), and sometimes with Latin as well. Overwhelmingly this evidence focuses on the South-West, but there is also some for the North-West and some for mid-Wales. It suggests settlement of some Irish, at least in the South-West, some time between the fourth and the seventh century, just as there was also Irish settlement in Cornwall and south-west Scotland at this time.[9] There is nothing to suggest settlement in any numbers in later centuries. Evidence for the political effects of this settlement is inconclusive but Irish and Welsh genealogies (which have twelve generations in common) indicate that it was believed by the tenth century that Déisi kings from south-east Ireland had ruled for several generations in south-west Wales; we have no hard evidence that this did happen but there is no reason why it should not have been so in the poorly evidenced early centuries. Richard White has also argued strongly for small territories ruled by Irish on Anglesey, at an early date, on the basis of regional names and hints of cultural affiliation.[10] Much later, in the early eleventh century, we certainly know of one Irishman, Rhain, who established himself as ruler in south-west Wales, and another, Turchil, who was killed in Wales in 1093; there were also at least two Irish overkings who claimed to rule the Welsh from Ireland in the eleventh century—Brian Boru and Diarmait mac Mael na mBó. Our evidence suggests, then, the presence of Irish people rather than Irish political institutions in Wales, although some, at some stages, were regarded as rulers.

[9] See Davies, *Wales*, 87–9; see also the map of 'Irish' inscriptions in Wales in B. Coplestone-Crow, 'The Dual Nature of the Irish Colonization of Dyfed in the Dark Ages', *Studia Celtica*, 16–17 (1981–2), 15.

[10] At the Early Church in Western Britain and Ireland Conference, Exeter, 1981; unfortunately this interesting paper was not included in the published conference proceedings. There is an undertow of Irishness, however, to his paper on the Arfryn cemetery, R. B. White, 'Excavations at Arfryn, Bodedern', *Anglesey Antiq. Soc. and Field Club Transactions* (1971–2), especially 42–51.

Irrespective of settlement and political control, there were clearly contacts over a long period between Ireland and Wales, cultural and religious contacts as well as political. We hear of people who moved between the two areas, like the British missionaries to Ireland of the fifth, sixth, and seventh centuries, and the Irishmen who came to the court of the ruler of north-west Wales in the early ninth century, as well as kings like Rhodri and Gruffudd ap Cynan. And we can observe the cultural influences in both directions of these and other personal con-tacts: thus we find north and south Welsh saints commemorated in later Irish martyrologies and common material (probably of Irish origin) in Welsh and Irish annals, as well as notice of Welsh events by Irish annalists; so also the Irish influences apparent on the sculptured crosses of Anglesey (Penmon es-pecially) of the Viking period.[11] Personal contacts and their influences were still clearly vital in the eleventh century: there is Irish material in eleventh-century Welsh Saints' Lives like those of Cadog and Dewi and in Welsh vernacular tales like 'Branwen', while the northern Welsh ruling dynasty of the eleventh century had very close contacts with people in Dublin. In short, contacts between west Wales and Ireland must have been frequent, if not the norm, and the early evidence seems to prefigure the establishment of a long-term pattern; there may even have been more Irish rulers in early medieval Wales than are evidenced in the surviving written sources. Arguments that Irish contacts were interrupted by Vikings in the ninth and tenth centuries are therefore not very convincing: plenty of Chester-made pottery reached Viking Dublin and the poem *Armes Prydein*, in the tenth century, calls upon the Scandinavians to *help* Welsh and other Britons expel the English from the island of Britain; while Rhodri Mawr (who could even have been Irish himself) naturally fled to Ireland from political troubles at home, even at the height of Scandinavian piracy.[12]

---

[11] See below, p. 55.

[12] See Davies, *Wales*, 174, 182, 196, 201; R. Sharpe, 'Gildas as a Father of the Church', in *Gildas: New Approaches*, ed. Lapidge and Dumville. David Dum-ville argued that the 'A' text of *Annales Cambriae* relied heavily on an Irish chronicle, perhaps created in the early tenth century, and that the 'B' and 'C' texts had a 'thickening' of Irish entries in late ninth and early tenth centuries, such that direct contact between St David's and Clonmacnoise was likely in the first half of the tenth century, Grabowski and Dumville, *Chronicles and Annals*,

WELSH POLITICAL RELATIONSHIPS, NINTH TO ELEVENTH CENTURIES

There are three aspects of political relationships within Wales which provoke comment: these are rulers and regions, the territorial range of rulers, and segmentation. To begin with rulers and regions: I have pointed out the preference of the Welsh Annals for the single ruler word *rex*, 'king', and for the virtual disappearance of this word from the Annals without substitution of any other term between 949 and 1018. In the eighth and ninth centuries there are frequent references to *reges*, with regions associated—king of Gwynedd, king of and in Ceredigion, and so on; the practice of naming kings and associating them with specific regions is rarer in the second half of the ninth century and first half of the tenth century (it is only used of Hywel Dda, Gwynedd kings, and non-Welsh kings); in the second half of the tenth century the word *rex* occurs once only—in 999—without territorial association; then in the third decade of the eleventh century the word comes into use again, although rarely and only occasionally with clear territorial associations.[13]

All this is so despite the fact that the territories themselves continue to be mentioned, but without associated kings; and despite the fact that many members of the royal dynasty of Gwynedd are noted, and doubtless retained their royal status, but without descriptive appellation. From the late ninth century, then, the prevailing mode of reference to those who exercised political authority was changing in the primary Latin political source. Members of the Gwynedd dynasty, for example, were present in Wales, and militarily and politically active; but they were not called kings of or in Gwynedd.

Now, as argued above, this must at least be a reflection of changing perceptions, a reflection of the way people (either a group or a succession of individuals) thought about things. But it may well be more than this. It is interesting that a strong sense of territorial identity was retained; however, the use of such

223–4. See also C. O'Rahilly, *Ireland and Wales* (London, 1924); P. Ó Riain, 'The Irish Element in Welsh Hagiographical Tradition', in *Irish Antiquity*, ed. D. Ó Corráin (Cork, 1981); cf. Huw Pryce's demonstration that a text of the eighth-century Irish collection of canons was available at an ecclesiastical centre in Wales in the early middle ages, 'Early Irish Canons', *Peritia*, 5 (1986).

[13] See above, p. 11; see also the comments of Davies, *Conquest, Coexistence, and Change*, 56–7.

identities for defining the bounds of political power disappeared by the year 1000. Moreover, in the eleventh century new terms for political spheres were used, especially (from 992) Latin *dextrales* (and *australes*) *Britones/dextralis patria* and vernacular *Deheubarth* for 'South Wales' (possibly foreshadowed by the word *Deheu* in the tenth-century *Armes Prydein*); correspondingly we find *Nortwallia* for 'the North' in 1039 and later, as also in the English *Domesday Book*.[14] If the new terms were coined to signify the territorial extent of the chief rulerdoms, then those rulerdoms no longer broadly corresponded to the principal regions of Wales.

Secondly, we may note the actual territorial range covered by rulers: most of the rulers noticed by the Welsh Annals in the period 1011–63, whatever the mode of reference to them, physically ranged over the whole of Wales; and a high proportion of the rulers of the earlier period 951–1011 ranged over all except the South-East. So, for example, the sons of Idwal (great grandsons of Rhodri Mawr) were in Montgomery, and then in Dyfed, and then Llanrwst, in the early 950s—Powys, Dyfed, Gwynedd; Maredudd ab Owain (great great grandson of Rhodri) was in Ceredigion and Dyfed (Cydweli), then went east to Glamorgan, then north to Gwynedd, in the years on either side of 1000; and Gruffudd ap Llywelyn was at Welshpool in the marches in the mid-eleventh century, then went right across Wales to Llanbadarn on the west coast, then south to the mouth of the Tywi and then back across Wales to Hereford (see Fig. 3). By contrast, the dominant pattern of ruler movements in the previous centuries (especially late seventh to mid-ninth) was characterized by confinement to one of the 'quarters' of Wales (north-west, south-west, south-east, north-east) or its borders.[15] In other words, from the mid-tenth century Welsh rulers tended to operate on a Wales-wide stage rather than on a limited regional stage (and in the eleventh century this extended even farther, into the English marches). The same changing pattern characterizes the range of Irish overkings at a slightly earlier period: until the mid-eighth century raiding and ranging tended

---

[14] *Annales Cambriae*, 992, 1023, 1039, 1049; cf. *Book of Llan Dâv*, 252 'per totam gualiam [1022]'; *Armes Prydein*, line 78; *Vita Cadoci*, ch. 24.

[15] This was not, of course, true of the early seventh century, when north Welsh kings ranged vast distances into midland and northern Britain.

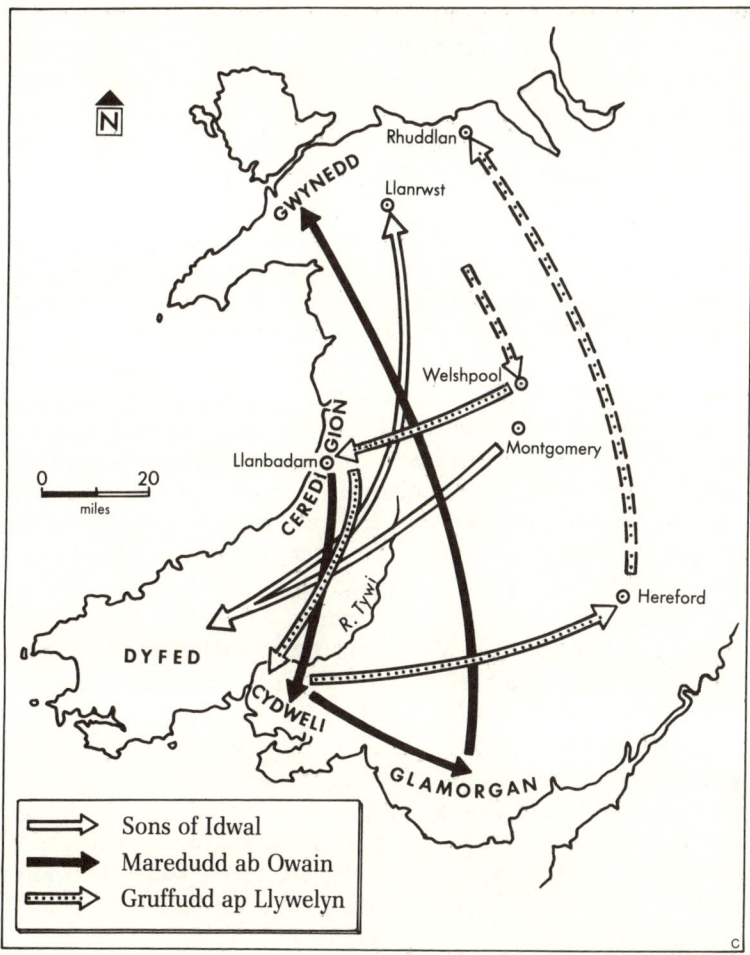

Fig. 3 Diagram of rulers' movements in the tenth and eleventh centuries

to be confined to one of the quarters of Ireland; from the late
eighth century kings raided more widely; and from the tenth
century the most powerful moved over the whole of Ireland,
seeking—ultimately—hegemony over the entire island. *Brut y
Tywysogyon*, with thirteenth-century hindsight, coined elabor-
ate titles for the wider-ranging Welsh rulers of the mid-tenth
century onwards: *goruchaf* ('highest [king]'), *pen a molyant*

('head and glory'), and so on.[16] These later rulers literally ranged over wide territories; they may well have sought some sort of political control of them (although there was little institutional machinery to support this); by the mid-eleventh century they were looking for hegemony over the whole of Wales as others across the water looked for hegemony over the whole of Ireland.

Thirdly, segmentation. It is perfectly clear that the transmission of political interest—whether Wales-wide or on a smaller scale—was dynastic: sons tended to succeed fathers or tried to do so; genealogies were recorded, in the tenth century or later, that traced descent. In these and other texts descent was viewed as one of the chief means of legitimizing rulership: if your father had been king you naturally had a claim to succeed him; consequently joint action by brothers, especially against cousins, and conflict between brothers over succession were common. Now, since the political interests of a ruling family were sustained from one generation to another, the number of interested individuals from any given dynasty tended to increase: the ruler had sons, who had sons, who had sons, and so on. Within two or three generations, therefore, five or six cousins might have an interest in one political sphere; they might *be* rulers, or fight battles for political control and try to be rulers. What happened in practice in the ninth, tenth, and eleventh centuries was that families segmented into branches, all claiming descent from a common, distant ancestor, although immediate interest groups were defined by reference to more recent ancestors; in the long term some branches dropped out of high-level politics, but several others might stay in, more usually competing with each other for political control than coming to any stabilizing arrangements.[17]

This phenomenon, of segmentation, is one of the principal determinants of the dynamic of tenth- and eleventh-century Welsh politics. In the South-East, for example, branches of the dynasty of Meurig ap Tewdrig shared and competed in the ninth as in the eleventh century. But it was the Gwynedd dynasty, the

[16] *Brut y Tywysogyon*, 949, 1022, 1063. These terms do not reflect the language of the more restrained contemporary Latin text, although the eleventh-century *reges* are more often *rex Brittonum*, 'king of the Britons' (i.e. Welsh), than *rex regionis*.

[17] See Davies, *Wales*, 124–5; and, for a classic comparison, D. Ó Corráin, 'Irish Regnal Succession', *Studia Hibernica*, 11 (1971).

descendants of Rhodri Mawr, that had the greatest impact on Wales. Effectively, segments—branches—of the Gwynedd dynasty came to have an interest in all parts of Wales, and came to conflict with each other in the course of trying to realize those interests.

Conflict between segments was already clear in Gwynedd in the early ninth century: at that time recorded conflict between Hywel and Cynan, both considered the descendants of Cunedda, focused on Anglesey. Conflict between segments became marked from the late ninth century, however, and was especially notable in the period between the mid-tenth and mid-eleventh centuries. Hence, we find the sons of Idwal fighting the sons of Hywel between 951 and 961, all great grandsons of Rhodri Mawr; and the sons of Idwal fighting each other in the early 970s; and their sons, the grandsons of Idwal, fighting each other in the years before 985. More distantly, Maredudd ab Owain fought the surviving grandson of Idwal (Cadwallon), his third cousin, both being great great grandsons of Rhodri Mawr; then, in 993, Maredudd fought his nephew Edwin; and in the next year he went against another branch of Idwal's grandsons, the sons of Meurig.[18]

The line of descent from Rhodri Mawr, from mid-ninth to the late eleventh century, has many branches and includes all but four of the principal named rulers in north- and south-west Wales (see Fig. 4). Although there is a broad distinction between the interests of the descendants of Rhodri's son Anarawd in the north and those of his son Cadell in the south-west, they did not confine themselves to north and south-west; witness the activities of the southern Maredudd, Gruffudd, and Rhiwallon in Gwynedd.[19] Several branches of this family sustained and pursued contemporary interests in the north in the mid-tenth century and in all parts in the mid-eleventh, as we have seen. In

[18] Any suggestion that Welsh royal succession practice depended on recognition of the equal rights of a four-generation kin-group, and that nomination of the successor was made from within that group, is in no way born out by tenth-century practice; nor any suggestion that by the late tenth century each king was nominating his successor, *pace* Binchy, *Celtic and Anglo-Saxon Kingship*, 25–30.

[19] Despite the late medieval antiquarian tradition that Rhodri 'divided' Wales between three of his sons; see Dumville, ' "Six" Sons of Rhodri Mawr', *Cambridge Medieval Celtic Studies*, 4 (1982), 11–12.

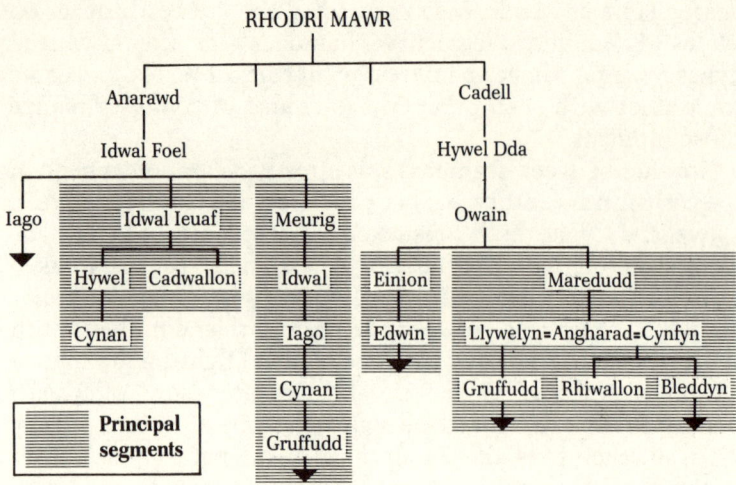

RHODRI MAWR

Fɪɢ. 4 Diagram to show descent from Rhodri Mawr and principal segments of the family

practice, then, although several contemporary annalists fix upon the great names of Hywel Dda and Gruffudd ap Llywelyn as powerful kings, what attracts them is an unusual territorial range, a dramatic military prowess.[20] Later historians picked this up, and emphasized their prominence, but what they ignore is the seething mass of competing political interests which is the context surrounding both Hywel and Gruffudd.

So to summarize: kingdoms were established in the fifth and sixth centuries, and some, perhaps, even slightly later; there were some changes in the framework so established but it essentially remained the same until the ninth century, with the kingdoms of the four 'corners' of Wales—each with its good lowland base—determining Welsh politics. Despite Rhodri Mawr and Hywel Dda, the traditional Welsh heroes of the ninth and tenth centuries, segmentation then began to dominate political history; in other words, interest in 'top' rulership was maintained by several branches of one family; they competed

[20] Cf. K. L. Maund, 'Cynan ab Iago and the Killing of Gruffudd ap Llywelyn', *Cambridge Medieval Celtic Studies*, 10 (1985), 57.

for that authority; and conflicted with each other in doing so. This, and the attempt to operate on a wider field, complicated by Viking intrusion, was too much for the undeveloped institutions of early medieval Wales. Thereafter, there was change in the way political power was exercised, described, and territorially defined; there were changes in political units and changes in perceptions; there was change in the pattern and structure of earlier relationships; and outsiders claimed more and more of a stake in the land, as we shall see below. By the early eleventh century political territorial consistency was lost, although territorial identities were to continue, and two new, larger, units—northern and southern—began to form. That they failed to get established is one of the chief problems of the century. Indeed, it is rather puzzling that Welsh politics developed in the way that they did; from the standpoint of the early post-Roman centuries, one might have expected otherwise. We have, then, a long-term development that seems to belie its origins, and an eleventh-century trend that quickly fizzles out. Some part of the answer to the problems posed by these failures must lie in external influences; it is to these that we must now turn.

4. Vikings

Wales was not, as may often be supposed, isolated in the early middle ages. Quite apart from the long-term Irish interaction, the ninth, tenth, and eleventh centuries were a period of notable English and Scandinavian interest in Wales. This brought Vikings and Englishmen to Wales and Welshmen to England and Ireland; journeys to eastern Ireland in this period took them to a Scandinavian sphere: Viking Dublin was founded in 841 and until the eleventh century was an essentially Scandinavian enclave.

VIKINGS

Irish Viking leaders, from Dublin and elsewhere, often played a significant part in Irish politics during the succeeding two hundred and fifty years. In 902, however, Viking leaders—following Ingimund—were expelled from Dublin and moved eastwards across the sea. It was not long before they were reinstated—some were back by 917—but their displacement had repercussions on the whole of the Irish Sea zone. Ingimund himself spent some time on Anglesey and may well have gone from there to the Wirral; others joined settlers on the west coast of Cumbria; others may have stayed on the Isle of Man.[1] A generation later, by the middle of the tenth century, some members of the Dublin community were as much absorbed in commerce as in Irish politics and for the next hundred and fifty years the northern European routes to Dublin—that is, west-wards from England via Chester and south from Scotland, the Isles, and Norway—were in constant use. The Irish Sea zone

---

[1] *Annals of Ulster*, 902; *Annales Cambriae*, 903. For the suggestion that the Norse settlement of the Wirral was in part fed from the Isle of Man, see G. Fellows-Jensen, 'Scandinavian Settlement in the Isle of Man and North-West England: The Place-Name Evidence', in *The Viking Age in the Isle of Man*, ed. C. Fell, P. Foote, J. Graham-Campbell, R. Thomson (London, 1983); see also J. Graham-Campbell, 'Tenth-Century Graves: The Viking-Age Artefacts from the Peel Castle Cemetery and their Significance', in D. Freke, *Peel Castle Excavations, 1982–7*, forthcoming, on the settlement of Man.

became in many ways a single—Scandinavianized—culture province, the Sea itself as populous and as focal as an inland lake (see Fig. 5).

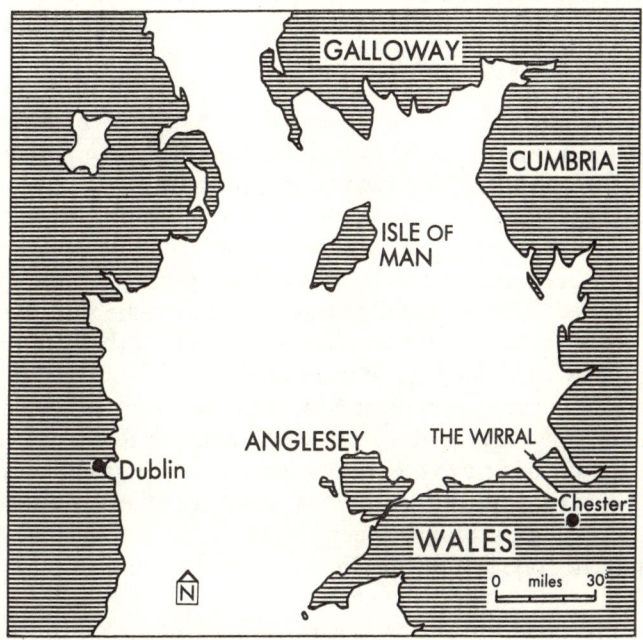

FIG. 5   The Irish Sea zone

By the late tenth century one area which had come to benefit from this activity was the Isle of Man, as the series of late tenth-century hoards of coins and other silver demonstrates; well positioned to dominate the Sea, it is an area richer in Hiberno-Norse coin finds than any part of Britain and contains almost as much ring-money (Scoto-Viking silver arm-rings of the period 925–1075) as the whole of Ireland.[2] Not surprisingly, up and coming rulers of the Hiberno-Scandinavian world sought to dominate sea-going activities from Man. The first that we hear of is Magnus son of Harold, a man who may well have been

[2] R. H. M. Dolley, 'The Palimpsest of Viking Settlement on Man', in *Proceedings of the Eighth Viking Congress*, ed. H. Bekker-Nielsen, P. Foote, O. Olsen (Odense, 1981); J. Graham-Campbell, 'The Viking-Age Silver Hoards of the Isle of Man', in *Viking Age in Man*, ed. Fell and others, 63.

displaced from Limerick when it was sacked by the Irish Dál Cais in 967. Within fifteen years Man was under attack from Earl Sigurd of the Orkneys and by 989 it was incorporated into the Orkney Earldom, although it certainly had its own local Scandinavian rulers or sub-rulers in the early eleventh century. Both Sigurd himself and Brodor of Man were killed in 1014 at the Irish battle of Clontarf, when Sitric of Dublin called on his Scandinavian allies to bring their fleets to assist the Leinster overking against the Irish superking Brian Boru. For fifty years thereafter connections between Dublin and Man became even closer in terms of material culture—someone may even have started to mint coins derived from Dublin types on Man—and this closeness may have had a political dimension too. One Olaf, called 'king' of Dublin, was thought by the mid-twelfth century to have ruled Man, Galloway, and north Wales too.[3] Eventually the kingdom of Man and the Isles entered a new phase; its alignments became firmly northern and the very close connections with Dublin were weakened, while Dublin itself looked increasingly to the south—southern Britain and western Europe—following the commercial trend from the early eleventh century onwards. Shipping continued to pass through the Irish Sea but the zone lost the distinctively unified character that had marked the tenth and eleventh centuries.

Viking raids on Wales began in the middle of the ninth century, with the killing of Cyngen in 852, and they are most notable in the second half of that century and second half of the tenth. The raids came mostly from the sea, with attacks focused on the south-western and north-western peninsulas, and Anglesey, although they sometimes went elsewhere. The

---

[3] Proceeding from the fact that he believed that there was a group of Hiberno-Manx coins, derived from the Hiberno-Norse coins of Dublin, of the 1030s, Dolley argued for a takeover of Man by one of the Dublin ruling family after 1014, 'The Pattern of Viking-Age Coin-Hoards from the Isle of Man', *Seaby's Coin and Medal Bulletin* (1975), 338–9; cf. Graham-Campbell, 'Silver Hoards of Man', in *Viking Age in Man*, ed. Fell and others, 62, 72. The numismatic connection (though not the interpretation) is incontrovertible; the political context arguable. The 'History' of Gruffudd ap Cynan, ch. 1, is quite explicit in its comments on Olaf; he may or may not have been 'king' of Dublin (certainly ruled by Sitric, Echmarcach, and Ivar in this period) but there is no reason to suppose that he did not belong to one of Dublin's ruling families; *Historia Gruffud vab Kenan*, ed. D. S. Evans (Cardiff, 1977), 1, 2 (38 and 47 for comment). See B. E. Crawford, *Scandinavian Scotland* (Leicester, 1987), 65–6, for Sigurd and Man.

first of many ravagings of Anglesey occurred in 877, but in the next year a Viking force wintered in Dyfed. A hundred years later, there was a string of raids on the monasteries of the west coast—961 Holyhead, 963 Tywyn, 971 Penmon, 978 Clynnog, 988 Llanbadarn, St Dogmaels, Llantwit, Lancarfan, and St David's—only one of many such attacks on the last. Armies also ranged across England from the east and south, touching the Welsh midlands, especially in the late ninth and early tenth centuries. The Danish army which had crossed England in 893 was defeated at Buttington, near Welshpool; it returned to Essex but re-formed to cross England again and harry the Welsh border in the succeeding years; twenty years later another party raiding up the Severn captured the bishop of south-west Herefordshire.[4]

VIKING SETTLEMENT

Raiding obviously has political consequences—at the least in concentrating available military resources—but I am less concerned here with the fact and effects of hit and run raids than with the possibility of continuing Scandinavian presence in Wales itself, and of action taken within Wales. The evidence for Scandinavian settlement in Wales has recently been reviewed by Henry Loyn and there is no need to repeat his detailed consideration.[5] In brief, he suggested that place-name evidence, even though much of it is coastal, is difficult to explain without accepting the presence of at least some Scandinavian speakers on the mainland of Wales. This place-name evidence concentrates on the south coast, especially the south-western coast, although it can also be found on the north coast and in Anglesey. Although we know that many of these names derive from maps—and that Welsh speakers used different, Welsh, names until recently—not all do so and other fragmentary indications of settlement reinforce Loyn's conclusions. There really must have been some permanent Scandinavian settlement in Wales, and we should not attach too much weight to the lack of explicit annalistic reference to it.

The Welsh Annals do however imply that Gruffudd ap

[4] See Davies, *Wales*, 116–17. For the aftermath of 893, cf. *Annales Cambriae*, 896, and Campbell and others, *Anglo-Saxons*, 151.
[5] H. R. Loyn, *The Vikings in Wales* (London, 1976).

Llywelyn got control of Scandinavians in north Wales, as of all others (including English), after 1039. Such fragmentary indications of settlement as there are suggest at least two foci in the north—in Anglesey and Arfon, across the Menai Straits, and in Tegeingl (Flint), west of the Dee near Prestatyn. In both areas the material evidence of the hoards and graves seems to me to have a qualitative value that is worthy of note. The hoards containing arm-rings, or arm-ring fragments, reflect a *distinctively* Scandinavian practice; they must have been collected by Scandinavians and it is exceptionally unlikely that they were deposited except by Scandinavians. Since a hoard was presumably hidden in the expectation that the depositor or his friends and family would return, it must indicate some familiarity with the land where it was deposited; whether or not the depositor was passing through, he expected to come back to the spot. A hoard of five silver arm-rings, collected within the outside limits of 850 and 930 (most probably in the early tenth century) was found in Dinorben Quarry, Llanfihangel Dinsilwy, Anglesey, and there is a Bangor-in-Arfon hoard of c.925—itself 'characteristically Scandinavian in coin composition'—which has arm-ring fragments; the Bangor hoard has characteristically Scandinavian silver ingots too.[6] These alone suggest some sort of Scandinavian presence in this north-western area in the early tenth century. The grave of a 'Viking' woman, buried with fragments of an antler comb, lies in a typically Viking burial site on a sandy ridge overlooking the sea, at Benllech on Anglesey; Anglesey itself has a Scandinavian name, Ongul's Isle; while, as we have seen, the mid-twelfth-century 'History' of Gruffudd ap Cynan claims that the Scandinavian Olaf ruled (in the early eleventh century) not only in Man and Galloway but on both sides of the Menai Straits, Anglesey and Gwynedd, where the earthworks of his 'castle' were still visible, called 'Bon y Dom'

---

[6] M. Blackburn and H. Pagan, 'A Revised Check-List of Coin Hoards from the British Isles, c. 500–1100', in *Anglo-Saxon Monetary History: Essays in Memory of Michael Dolley*, ed. M. A. S. Blackburn (Leicester, 1986), no. 106; cf. also no. 98, a small Anglesey hoard of c.915. S. Kruse, 'Ingots and Weight Units in Viking Age Silver Hoards', *World Archaeology*, 20 (1988), 290–1. I am extremely grateful to my colleague James Graham-Campbell for giving me his opinion on the arm-rings, for which see also G. C. Boon, *Welsh Hoards 1979–1981* (Cardiff, 1986), 98–102.

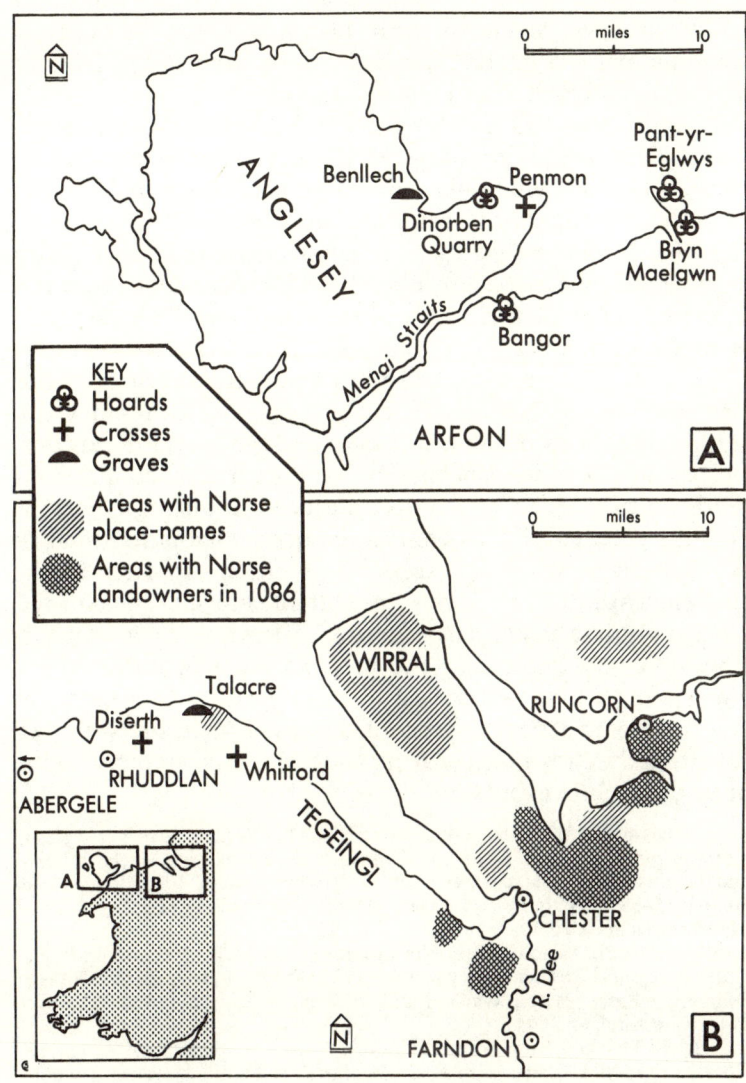

Fig. 6 Viking presence in (*a*) north-west Wales, (*b*) north-east Wales

in Welsh (see Fig. 6). The large hoard of 204 coins deposited *c*.1024 at Bryn Maelgwn, near Llandudno (and Degannwy) contains many coins of Cnut and one of Sitric of Dublin and may equally reflect Scandinavian activity.[7]

Tegeingl also has a Viking grave—at Talacre—which included a spearhead; from Llys Awel, near Abergele to the west, comes a pseudo-penannular brooch from a 'Viking *milieu*'; the English *Domesday Book* records a few Scandinavian names in the area, at least indicating Scandinavian-speaking ownership of properties there (see Fig. 6).[8] This area was not far from the Scandinavian settlement zone of the Wirral and Chester, and is in many ways a natural extension of that. Vikings came into Chester in 893 and, although the English took control of the city again in 907, it is perfectly clear that Scandinavians continued to be in and about Chester through the tenth century, at least in the context of the Dublin commercial connection; tenth-century levels at Chester are now producing plenty of Dublin-type material, as well as the occasional pure Scandinavian artefact, while Chesterware is prolific in later tenth- and eleventh-century levels in Dublin and Chester-minted coins dominate Irish hoards up to 975; the hoard deposited in Chester *c*.965 looks like the property of a Scots or Manx Norseman. Viking settlement of the Wirral, well attested by place-name evidence, and recorded in Irish tradition, seems to date from the early tenth century and may be in part consequent upon the Dublin expulsions of 902.[9]

[7] N. Edwards, 'A Possible Viking Grave from Benllech, Anglesey', *Anglesey Antiquarian Society and Field Club Transactions* (1985). Bryn Maelgwn hoard and the possibly associated, small, Pant-yr-Eglwys hoard of *c*.1023: Boon, *Welsh Hoards*, 1–35; Blackburn and Pagan, 'Revised Check-List', in *Anglo-Saxon Monetary History*, ed. Blackburn, nos. 208, 207.

[8] F. G. Smith, 'Talacre and the Viking Grave', *Proceedings of the Llandudno, Colwyn Bay and District Field Club*, 17 (1931–3); J. M. Lewis, 'Recent Finds of Penannular Brooches from Wales', *Medieval Archaeology*, 26 (1982); *Domesday Book* (Cheshire), fo. 269a.

[9] A. T. Thacker, 'Anglo-Saxon Cheshire', in *A History of the County of Chester*, 1, ed. B. E. Harris with A. T. Thacker (VCH; Oxford [for IHR London], 1987), 254–8; Graham-Campbell, 'Silver Hoards of Man', in *Viking Age in Man*, ed. Fell and others, 69–70, and id., 'Two Scandinavian Disc Brooches of Viking Age Date from England', *Antiquaries Journal*, 65 (1985). I am very grateful to Alan Thacker for allowing me to see a text of his VCH chapter in advance of publication, as also to Peter Carrington of the Grosvenor Museum Chester for many helpful discussions on recent archaeological work in Chester. See below, n. 12, for references to settlement in the Wirral.

Viking arm-rings from Dinorben Quarry, Anglesey
(*by kind permission of the National Museum of Wales*)

In both areas, although they are not in themselves evidence of any particular sort of settlement, we should not forget the sculptured stones decorated with characteristically Scandinavian motifs; whether we believe that they were created to cater for local Scandinavian tastes, or for local tastes influenced by Scandinavian fashions, or that they were decorated by sculptors who simply drew on a wide range of motifs known to them, they are witness to closely localizable Scandinavian influence. Some of the stones of north Wales, from Penmon, Diserth, and Whitford, share characteristics with a group surrounding the Irish Sea, a group whose very existence is witness to the cultural interconnections of the Irish Sea coasts in the tenth century.[10] They emphasize the fact that north Wales belonged to this Irish Sea culture zone.

There must also have been some settlement in south Wales. There are 'Scandinavian' motifs on the Penally, Nevern, and Carew crosses but the hoards are small and not distinctively Viking; one might look for settlement evidence in the Tywi, Neath, Taff, or Usk estuaries and in Gower and Pembroke, but relevant evidence is much more scattered and much more difficult to localize than that of the north. There is no striking concurrence of indicators.[11]

The indications above are not of very high quality as *evidence*, and none would stand alone as an undeniable pointer to Scandinavian settlement in Wales; however, they are consistent and reinforce each other. Both parts of the north have the sheltered landing-places, in the Menai Straits and Dee estuary, that the

[10] R. N. Bailey, *Viking Age Sculpture in Northern England* (London, 1980), 177–82; *ECMW*, nos. 37, 38, 185, 190; cf. J. E. Clarke, 'Welsh Sculptured Crosses and Cross-Slabs of the Pre-Norman Period', Ph.D. thesis (2 vols.; University College London, 1981), 1. 204, 2. 143–4. I am very grateful to Nancy Edwards for her comments on these crosses; she remarks that the Penmon crosses show links with those of Scandinavian areas of settlement in the Wirral, Cumbria, and the Isle of Man but also that the iconography and abstract ornament are paralleled by a group of crosses centred on the Barrow Valley in Ireland; the important point is that their associations are decidedly multicultural.

[11] There are plenty of suggestions, however, in B. G. Charles, *Old Norse Relations with Wales* (Cardiff, 1934); and Alan Lane points to some slight concentration of evidence in Gower, 'The Vikings in Glamorgan?', in *Glamorgan County History*, 2, ed. H. N. Savory (Cardiff, 1984), 355; see also the 'ball-type' brooch from Culver Hole, J. Graham-Campbell, 'Some Viking-Age Penannular Brooches', in *From the Stone Age to the 'Forty-Five*, ed. A. O'Connor and D. V. Clarke (Edinburgh, 1983), 316.

sea-going Vikings would have needed. This need not imply any very large groups of settlers; indeed, it is absolutely clear that the amount of Scandinavian-influenced material (and names) is relatively small; there simply isn't the material that occurs in the Isle of Man, to take a near example. Scandinavian settlement in north Wales must therefore have been thin, and we have no need to think in terms of more than a few small communities; any suggestion of Viking urban settlements, such as developed in Ireland, is distinctly lacking. All of the indicators would place this northern settlement in the first half of the tenth century: the Bangor hoard dates to *c.*925; the Anglesey arm-rings are most unlikely to have been deposited later than 930; the graves are unlikely to be later than 950 and the stones than the mid-tenth century; the Scandinavianization of Chester began early in the century. By contrast, there is a notable absence of distinctively Scandinavian material of later date.

VIKING RULERS

The issue of Scandinavian political presence in Wales is also tricky, although it is not the same as that of settlement pure and simple: the few settlers of the early tenth century had no necessary connection with the Viking leaders acting in Wales in the late tenth and early eleventh centuries.

When Vikings forced Rhodri Mawr overseas to Ireland in 876 it was presumably a land-based force that caused this degree of trouble. A little later, in 902 or 903, we know that Ingimund established himself on Anglesey, in Osfeilion, near Llanfaes, although tradition has it that he soon moved on to the Chester area.[12] As mentioned above, a mid-twelfth-century text chronicling Gruffudd's activities, the 'History' of Gruffudd ap Cynan, refers to the belief that Olaf of Dublin (Gruffudd's mother's father) ruled in Anglesey and mainland Gwynedd in the early eleventh century (as well as Man and Galloway); and the Irish overkings who took control of Dublin in the eleventh century claimed with that the power to rule British (i.e. Welsh) too: it looks as if the political powers associated with rule of Dublin at

---

[12] *Annales Cambriae*, 903; F. T. Wainwright, 'Ingimund's Invasion', *English Historical Review*, 63 (1948); *Fragmentary Annals of Ireland*, ed. J. N. Radner (Dublin, 1978), 168–72, and see also 206–7.

that time included some nominal control of north Wales.[13] In any case, we know that Rhodri's descendant, Cynan ab Iago, had close personal contacts with the Scandinavian community of Dublin; he married Olaf's daughter and had his son Gruffudd brought up there. So, the Vikings seem to have been campaigning in north Wales in the later ninth century, stopping in Anglesey in the early tenth, but in some sense ruling in the North-West by the early eleventh. There is no evidence, nor trace, however, of distinctive Scandinavian *polities*: we do not find any Welsh equivalent of the Scandinavian kingdoms of York or Dublin, distinctive enclaves with a hinterland, but an uncertain (and probably fluctuating) political relationship with that hinterland.

In the light of Scandinavian activity in the Irish Sea province in the second half of the tenth century, I think we need to rethink the relationship of Scandinavian leaders to north-west Wales at that time. This was a period of regular raiding of Welsh monasteries, that is of identifiable resource centres; viewed from another perspective, it was a period of regular tribute-taking by those with the greatest political power—who happened to be Scandinavian. The tribute consequent upon raiding was sometimes clearly identified as such by the annalists: reference to the taking of a *census* seems to lie behind the records of the 972 raid on Anglesey; slaves were taken from Anglesey in 987; and Maredudd ab Owain paid a well-known tribute to the 'Black Gentiles' of (perhaps) a penny a head in 989.[14] The tribute-takers may have had a base within Wales or without, or both; wherever, they had effective political power in north-west Wales and tribute went to them rather than to any Welsh leader. This is absolutely explicit in the case of Maredudd's 989 tax: in that year Maredudd, the most powerful Welsh leader of the time, helpfully made the collection for his political overlords.[15]

---

[13] *Annals of Ulster*, 1014; 'The Annals of Tigernach', ed. W. Stokes, *Revue Celtique*, 17 (1896), 410 (s.a. 1072: Diarmait mac Mael na mBó, king of Britons, the Hebrides, Dublin, and the southern half of Ireland).

[14] *Brut y Tywysogyon, Peniarth MS. 20 Version*, 972; see T. Jones's note to the translation, 143.

[15] *Brut y Tywysogyon*, 987, if not garbled, could be taken to imply that power was shared between the sons of Harold and Maredudd, for the Peniarth MS. 20 version seems to suggest that after Godfrey took thousands of slaves on

Now, it is evident that more than one Viking group had interests in north-west Wales and that one of those groups also had interests in control of the Isle of Man. Some raiders of Wales are simply called 'gentiles' and may or may not be identifiable with one of the known groups. The Dublin sons of Olaf were involved in raiding Llŷn in 961, but it was the sons of Harold— ousted from Limerick, perhaps, in 967 but certainly entrenched on Man till 982–9—who are named again and again in the period 971–87. Moreover, at least the sons of Harold became involved in the tortuous segmentary politics of Gwynedd in the late 970s: Hywel allied with Vikings in 978;[16] his uncle Iago, whom Hywel had expelled four years earlier, was killed by Vikings in 979; and Iago's son Cystennin used the sons of Harold against Llŷn and Anglesey in the following year, only to meet his own death at the hands of Hywel (or his forces). In other words, the Man Vikings were heavily involved in the political battles for control of Anglesey—the focus of political power in Gwynedd— in the years running up to 980. They also remained very active in Anglesey through the 980s—that is, at the very time when they were being challenged for control of Man by Sigurd (which they were to lose by the end of the decade).

It therefore seems extremely likely that the Man-based sons of Harold were effectively controlling Gwynedd in the 970s and 980s; and may even have had bases on Anglesey in the 980s. We do not know where they went after Sigurd secured his hold on Man but they may have kept their interests in Wales and, even if not, Sigurd may have inherited their association with Gwynedd. The Isle of Man/Gwynedd connection still seems to have been there in the early eleventh century, when Olaf 'ruled', although by then there was a Dublin slant to the association and Dublin overkings were liable to claim powers over Wales too. At least some branches of the Gwynedd dynasty also kept in close touch with Dublin.[17] By 1039, however, the situation was changing in

Anglesey, Maredudd took some too and went home to Dyfed. However, if so, Maredudd's success was very short-lived. On slave-trading as an aspect of Hiberno-Norse tribute, and a very important one in the Irish Sea province in the eleventh century, see P. Holm, 'The Slave Trade of Dublin', *Peritia*, 5 (1986), 341–3.

[16] See below, p. 77, n. 30.

[17] As others were to do throughout the eleventh and twelfth centuries; see Davies, *Conquest, Coexistence, and Change*, 10–11.

Wales: Gruffudd ap Llywelyn came up from the south and seems to have established himself in Gwynedd; Cynan ab Iago fled to Dublin; Gruffudd got control of the Scandinavians (as well as others) in Wales and went on to range impressively throughout Wales in the next twenty years. The claims of Dublin overkings to rule the Welsh became outdated—and as meaningless as the claim to rule the Isles and Shetland.

In effect, then, Scandinavians were controlling Gwynedd—or large parts of it—between about 960 and 1025. Plenty of segments of the Gwynedd dynasty had an active interest in Gwynedd in this period, and some were regarded by the annalists as 'holding' Gwynedd; but they weren't called kings of Gwynedd, they were often in conflict with each other, and they paid tribute to the Vikings. Maredudd ab Owain may have made a successful foray from the south in 986, but within a year he was returning to Dyfed and within three he was paying tribute himself. Moreover, the Irish Annals of Ulster name the Strathclyde king as *rí Bretan*, 'king of the Britons', in 975, although normally—outside the period 949–1023—they applied this impressive term to a Welsh king, especially the king of Gwynedd. It is also worth considering the Scandinavian Sigferth (Syferð) who was named with Welsh kings at the English king Eadred's court in 955 and later by Florence of Worcester among the kings who rowed King Edgar on the River Dee—along with Hywel and Iago of the line of Rhodri, and Magnus son of Harold; was this because he too was a north Welsh king?[18]

If Scandinavians ruled Gwynedd in this period it does not have to mean the establishment of a distinctive polity: we do not have to postulate a Scandinavian kingdom of Bangor; it may not even mean the establishment of an alternative polity, with Scandinavian kings of Gwynedd substituted for the regular Welsh line of Rhodri Mawr. Scandinavian presence and military power, backed by a capacity to range across the Irish Sea, and the Scandinavian ability to take tribute, may merely have made the effective continuation of a Welsh polity impossible.[19]

[18] W. de Gray Birch, *Cartularium Saxonicum* (4 vols.; London, 1885–99), 3, no. 909; see P. H. Sawyer, *Anglo-Saxon Charters* (London, 1968), no. 566. Florence of Worcester, *Chronicon ex Chronicis*, ed. B. Thorpe (2 vols.; London, 1848–9), 1. 142–3.

[19] Peter Sawyer comments that kingship in Scandinavia characteristically involved many lesser kings (*jarls*) who paid tribute to a few great kings, a

'Scandinavian rule' may well have meant Viking bases in Wales for a time; it certainly meant Viking fighters in Wales, both fighting against the Welsh and for the Welsh, for they provided a new pool of soldiers for Welsh kings;[20] but it did not *have* to mean permanent settlement. The leaders of the late tenth and eleventh centuries may have left few or no heirs in Wales.

small-scale multiple kingship structure in which the passage of tribute was crucial; *The Making of Sweden* (Alingsås, 1988), 3–4. In Gwynedd in the later tenth century, whatever the identity and the ethnicity of the local ruler, the tribute was channelled off to some greater king; this certainly fits the Scandinavian pattern. Cf. Crawford, *Scandinavian Scotland*, 91, on the precocious development of taxation systems by the Norse in Scotland and the Isles.

[20] A development important in itself, which had major repercussions; see further below, p. 77, 87–8.

5. The Welsh and the English

The English came to Britain in the late fourth, fifth, and sixth centuries in the course of a major population movement from the continent; they settled predominantly in the south and east of the island, but within the early middle ages took political control of the whole area included in the present kingdom of England. Western and northern parts of England always remained rather thinly sprinkled with people of Germanic stock but— whatever the density of settlement—the language of the settlers came to predominate, replacing the indigenous Brittonic speech. The speed and type of political domination were not always closely related to the speed and density of settlement. However, it is broadly true to say that all but Cornwall was controlled by the English by the early eighth century, leaving the British in control there for another century (as they were in southern Scotland until the early eleventh century and Wales until the late thirteenth). Although English control was initially organized as a complex of small independent kingdoms, the long-term trend was for the amalgamation of small units into more powerful blocks. This process ultimately reached its logical conclusion, partly hindered and partly assisted by the contest with the Vikings in the ninth and tenth centuries, with the establishment—by the West Saxon dynasty—of a single consolidated kingdom of England. This kingdom was essentially a creation of the tenth century, a period of quite remarkable sophistication in the processes of English government and in the development of fiscal and administrative machinery; it was also a period in which the political capacity of the English kings increased enormously and, not content with the incorporation of Cornwall into the kingdom, they began to look to western and northern parts of the island. Though government always remained firmly based in the south, the kings of England mounted expeditions north as well as west and entered into relationships with the leaders on their frontiers. For a time it looked as if they were set to become masters of the whole island, and for a time in the mid-tenth century they used titles suggesting that they already did so—'king of the whole of Britain/Albion', 'king of the English, pagans, and all peoples of the island'—but the rapidly changing political situation of the kingdom and of the Scandinavian world diverted attention from these ambitions by the early eleventh century.[1]

In fact the Welsh were often affected by these processes, but there were especially critical phases for them in the seventh century, with the political takeover of the midlands, and in the tenth century, with the extension of the English kings' interests and rapid development of their machinery of government. However, the English interaction with Wales was more complicated than the confrontation of the British by an ever advancing aggressor: we should not suppose that the English were simply lined up on the other side of the border, waiting to take Wales. The English were often in Wales, they had power there, and they were involved in Welsh politics. To appreciate the complexity of this force in Welsh affairs, we need to look more closely at 'the border', at English political control in Wales, and at English alliances.

THE ENGLISH BORDER

In the English midlands the western limits of English political control were broadly determined by the late seventh century, in the area of the present English–Welsh boundary: early in the seventh century in the south (along the course of the River Wye); and during the second and third quarters of the seventh century in the centre (north-western Herefordshire and western Shropshire). Most modern opinion sees this as a 'peaceful' process, following the views of place-name scholars who, pointing to the intermingling of Welsh and English names at an early date, suggest gradually extending English settlement and peaceful co-existence.[2] They may or may not be right about peaceful

---

[1] For English political development see F. M. Stenton, *Anglo-Saxon England* (3rd edn.; Oxford, 1971), Campbell and others, *Anglo-Saxons*, and countless surveys; for British speech and names Jackson, *Language and History in Early Britain*; for English royal titles E. John, *Orbis Britanniae* (Leicester, 1966), 49–56.
[2] The seminal work comes in H. P. R. Finberg, *The Early Charters of the*

settlement; but the peacefulness of the settlement does not tell us much about political control. The literature relating to seventh-century Shropshire, at least, presents the Welsh as aggrieved losers in a lengthy battle;[3] rulers may well have fought all along the line; it was rulers, after all, who had things to lose. Now, although—for the most part— there was little subsequent change to this seventh-century disposition of political spheres, what happened in the northern border area in the late sixth and seventh centuries was much less of a determinant for the future.[4] It is clear that the English did not swamp the British of Cheshire in the sixth and seventh centuries: there was a significant Welsh-speaking population in Cheshire after the sixth century. It is also clear that the battle of Chester of 616 did not separate the English from the Welsh and the Welsh from their British brothers to the north; it was not the decisive occasion that older generations of historians supposed. The battle may have dislodged a Welsh dynasty (quite possibly the Cadelling) from a political base in Chester, but it did not immediately replace it with an English one. We do not know of an

West Midlands (Leicester, 1961), 197–224, and id., 'Mercians and Welsh', in his *Lucerna* (London, 1964), but there is plenty of subsequent comment; see, for example, M. Gelling, 'The Early History of Western Mercia', and K. Pretty, 'Defining the Magonsaete', in *The Origins of Anglo-Saxon Kingdoms*, ed. S. Bassett (London, 1989). Kate Pretty credibly suggests a much more complex process than heretofore.

[3] Summarized in Davies, *Wales*, 99–102. I think this remains more useful than Gelling's account in Bassett, *Origins of Anglo-Saxon Kingdoms*, 188–91; earlier in the same work Nicholas Brooks treats the same material more clearly (and, surprisingly, differently), ibid. 168–9. Jenny Rowland's recent work, on which they both depend, raises the possibility that Mercian conquest of Shropshire did not take place till the eighth century; this is conceivable, although a seventh-century date still seems to me to be more likely (even if late seventh century). I take her point that the poem 'Marwnad Cynddylan', relating to the early to mid-seventh century, need not be a lament about the English conquest of (English) Powys, but some other disaster; and that 'Canu Heledd' derives its poignancy from its ninth-century perspective and does not constitute 'evidence' that the mid-Welsh kings' loss of Shropshire must be tied to the death of Cynddylan in the mid-seventh century. Her association of the construction of Wat's Dyke with a conquest of Shropshire in the mid-eighth century is at the moment quite incredible to me (see further below, p. 65, 73); J. Rowland, 'A Study of the Saga Englynion', Ph.D. thesis (University of Wales, 1982), 1. 299–362, especially 338–40, 341, 350.

[4] Although the northern part of Ergyng (south-west Herefordshire) seems to have become English dominated some time shortly after c.850–74; see Davies, *Microcosm*, 26.

early English kingdom of Cheshire to compare with those of Shropshire and Herefordshire, Gloucestershire, the Midlands, and so on.[5] Significantly, there is nothing which suggests that the present western boundary of Cheshire—the northernmost part of the modern Welsh boundary—even roughly represents any seventh- (or seventh- to twelfth-) century political boundary. Indeed, by contrast, it is clear that the lands administered from Chester in the twelfth century included areas west of the present boundary (see Fig. 10).[6] In this area, then, English/Welsh political spheres and the border zone were *not* defined in the seventh century.

Secondly, Offa's Dyke: it is conventional, following the seminal work of Sir Cyril Fox, to see the Dyke as a boundary between English and Welsh, running from 'sea to sea', constructed by the Mercian king Offa, in the late eighth century. Fox saw it as a frontier agreed between Welsh and English, with gaps along its course so that passage from east to west and vice versa might be controlled.[7] It remains a very impressive monument in the middle border area, although there is nothing now to be seen in the northernmost sector of Fox's line; moreover, there is nothing across Ergyng (south-west Herefordshire); and nothing for much of the southernmost sector—except a curious bank high on the cliffs above the Wye. In the last generation David Hill's work has modified much of the conventional interpretation. It has become clear that the Dyke is not a unitary work: its structure varies and some sections are of earlier origin than others. It does not continue to the north coast, neither on Fox's suggested line nor on other possible ones; it does not exist across Ergyng nor in the south; it is not a frontier with control points: many of the apparent

---

[5] See J. McN. Dodgson, 'The English Arrival in Cheshire', *Trans. Historic Society of Lancashire and Cheshire*, 119 (1967), 29–32; see also A. T. Thacker, *VCH Chester*, 1. 242–3. *Annales Cambriae*, 613 (= 616); Bede, *Historia Ecclesiastica*, 2. 2; Davies, *Wales*, 94.

[6] John Dodgson thought that the name Tarvin (signifying 'boundary') must have represented some early political boundary, *Trans. Hist. Soc. Lancs. and Chesh.*, 119 (1967), 32, 36, but there is no need to assume that it was political; see Thacker, *VCH Chester*, 1. 242. Cf. Davies, *Conquest, Coexistence, and Change*, 3–4.

[7] Sir Cyril Fox, *Offa's Dyke* (London, 1955).

Offa's Dyke, Llanfiar Waterdine
(*by kind permission of The Clwyd-Powys Archaeological Trust*)

gaps are not original and all except one of the suggested gateways that have been tested have been shown to be relatively recent.[8]

Hence, the present monument is not so complete a boundary and not so purely the product of a single master plan. However, 'Wat's Dyke' in the north, running from the Severn to Holywell, to the east of Offa's Dyke and of Fox's postulated northern section, constitutes in effect a northward extension of the Dyke and takes it to the coast (see Fig. 7).[9] There remains no dating evidence of construction for either (nor any conclusive evidence of function, although the westward-facing ditch of Offa's Dyke must suggest some sort of 'defensive' function against the Welsh). Hence, the assumption that here is a Wales-long barrier, constructed in the late eighth century, standing through the ninth/tenth/eleventh centuries and thereafter, simply cannot be sustained. We do not know when the sections of pre-existing dyke across the midlands were linked and we do not know when Wat's Dyke was added. Given Asser's comment in the late ninth century that Offa built a dyke from sea to sea between Britain (i.e. Wales) and Mercia, we may as well for the moment attribute the linking to Offa in the late eighth century; but Asser's 'sea to sea' comment—at least—is patently incorrect and might at best be interpreted as 'river to river', perhaps Clwyd to Wye although there are other possibilities. Wat's Dyke is a different matter: it is a different structure and it simply does not follow that its construction was contemporary with the linking of the Offa's

[8] There are a few brief publications (e.g., recently, D. Hill, *Medieval Archaeology*, 30 (1986), 150–3; id., 'The Construction of Offa's Dyke', *Antiquaries Journal*, 65 (1985), 140–2) but David Hill's most sustained treatment of the problems has come in talks and lectures; especially useful talks that I have attended include those to the Archaeological Association, London, February 1982, and to medieval archaeologists in UCL, March 1988. (Since I wrote this book David Hill has kindly sent me a draft copy of his book, *Offa's and Wat's Dykes*, and I therefore have been able to benefit from reading a *very* sustained treatment. This substantial work deserves consideration on its merits and I hope it will be published soon; for the moment, readers may like to know that Dr Hill would opt for a construction date for Offa's Dyke in the 770s and for Wat's Dyke in the 850s, all things considered; however, the detail of his treatment, as well as his own discussion of the limitations of the evidence, needs full attention.)

[9] D. Hill, *Medieval Archaeology*, 25 (1981), 184; id., *Med. Arch.*, 30 (1986), 150, 151; and personal comments.

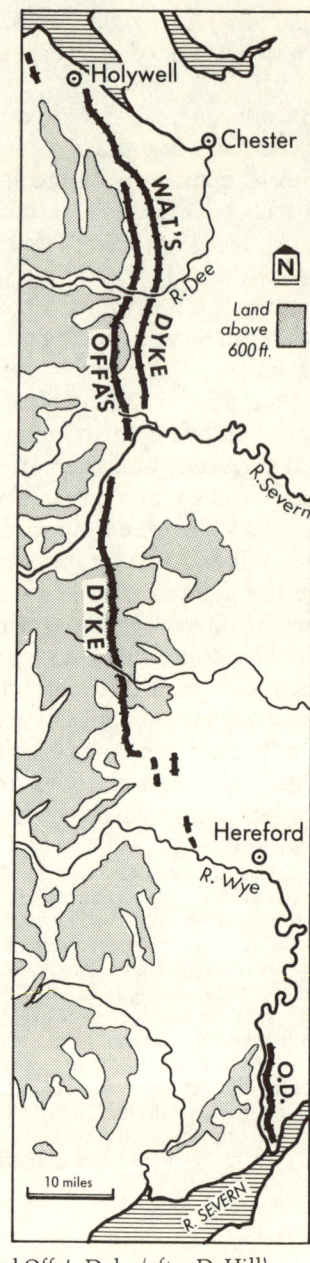

Fɪɢ. 7   Wat's Dyke and Offa's Dyke (after D. Hill)

Dyke sections.[10] It must therefore remain possible, if not likely, that the western limit of the English sphere in the north was *not* defined on the ground in the eighth century and that passage to north-west Wales remained open through the ninth century and perhaps beyond. North-eastern Wales was not therefore cut off from the English north-west midlands by 800. The idea that the unit 'Wales', roughly as we know it now, was territorially defined in the very early middle ages, and cut off from the English midlands in the later eighth century, will not stand.

ENGLISH CONTROL OF WALES

Even more inappropriate is the notion that the creation of Offa's Dyke was 'to put a stop to the apparently successful Welsh counterattack'.[11] The overwhelming tenor of the surviving written evidence is that it was the English who repeatedly launched attacks on Wales, and not the Welsh who attacked England. Despite popular belief, schoolbooks, and the mythology that surrounds the Dyke, it is extremely difficult to find solid evidence of Welsh attacks on the English between the late seventh and mid-eleventh centuries. On the contrary, both Welsh *and* English sources record English attacks on the Welsh, led by English kings, especially Mercian, in the eighth and ninth centuries, and by English ealdormen and sheriffs in the tenth and eleventh centuries. Even in the late eleventh century, *Domesday Book*'s 'customs' of Hereford include an obligation on the men of Hereford to accompany the English sheriff on expedition to Wales; by then, raiding was so normal it had become institutionalized.[12] These raids were both short range and long range, from King Aethelbald nibbling at the border zone in Ergyng in the early eighth century to Cenwulf or Offa piercing into the heart of south-west Dyfed or north-west

---

[10] Although in November 1987 David Hill thought that the structure of Wat's Dyke was 'not unlike' some parts of Offa's Dyke, at that stage this was not firm enough to propose contemporaneity; others working on Wat's Dyke in the last decade have in any case identified structural differences between its different sections, *Archaeology in Wales*, 24 (1984), 66–7 (NB J. Rowland's suggestion of an *earlier* date for Wat's Dyke: above, n. 3). *Asser's Life of King Alfred*, ch. 14.

[11] P. Wormald in Campbell and others, *Anglo-Saxons*, 121.

[12] *Domesday Book* (Herefordshire), fo. 179a.

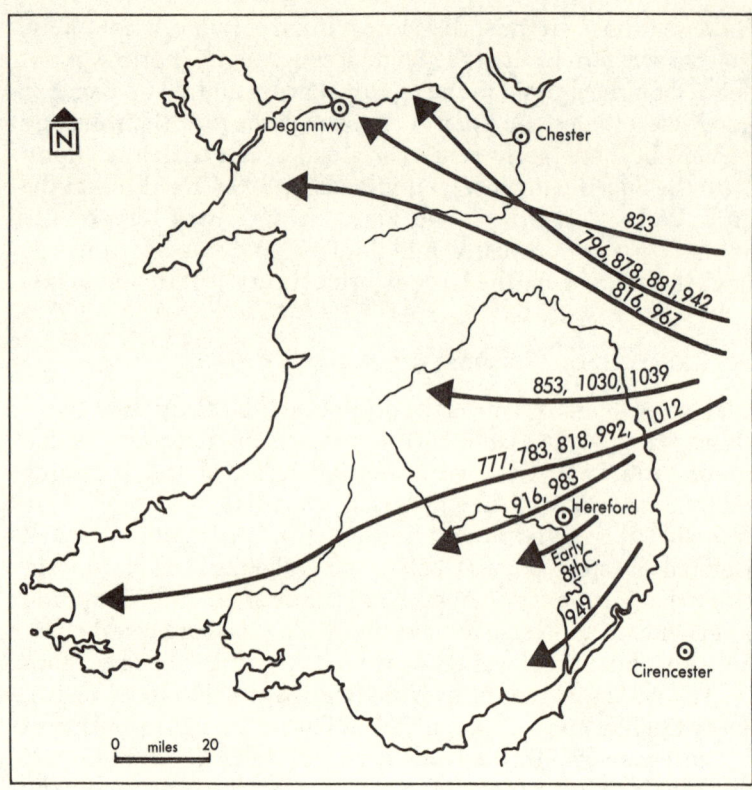

FIG. 8   English attacks on Wales

Gwynedd, in the later eighth century, as others later too (Fig. 8).
There are many of them. I therefore think that there was a
consistent tendency for the English, especially the midland
English, to raid Wales; a major aspect of English/Welsh relationships was sustained political conflict, with the English as
aggressors. The tables were certainly turned in the mid-eleventh
century, when Gruffudd ap Llywelyn raided the borders sys-
tematically, doubtless with specific political objectives in mind.[13]
But this was a very particular and new situation. For the rest, we
should not be misled by the Anglo-centric historiography.

[13] See Lewis, 'English and Norman Government and Lordship in the Welsh
Borders, 1039–1087', 131; cf. Maund, 'Cynan ab Iago and the Killing of Gruffudd
ap Llywelyn', *Camb. Med. Celt. Stud.*, 10 (1985), 59.

English aggression was not merely a question of raids on Wales; a substantial proportion of present north Wales must in fact have been controlled by the English in the ninth century, as Lloyd himself pointed out: already in 796 we have notice of the English fighting at Rhuddlan on the River Clwyd, a site later (921) fortified by them as part of the midland English burghal system; by 816 the English were fighting well to the west in Snowdonia and the manner of reference to that fighting (*invaserunt*, 'invaded') suggests a campaign rather than a raid; by then they had conquered Rhufoniog and by 823 they had 'destroyed' Degannwy, a major stronghold on the Conwy, taking the kingdom of Powys 'into their power', as the annalist says (see Fig. 9). Degannwy was no isolated hillfort; it was a political centre; kings of Powys survived another generation but not beyond 855. Some time later, in 878, Rhodri Mawr of Gwynedd and his son were killed by the English, who were themselves defeated at the Conwy a couple of years after this.[14] The English were undoubtedly campaigning *in* north Wales for much of the ninth century. To campaign this far west they must have controlled the lowland base of north-east Wales (i.e. west Cheshire, Flint (Tegeingl), and the narrow coastal strip of north Wales), and this may well have extended farther at times, at least to the Conwy.

The Vikings came into Chester in 893 and upset all this. As a consequence, from the 890s the situation becomes more difficult to characterize (see Fig. 6b). Just as the political status of the English midlands became extremely variable, scored by military campaigns and claimed now by one side, now by another, so north-east Wales (as a western extension of the midlands) shared the instability and the problems. Though the Vikings were controlling the East Midlands by the 870s, in the West Midlands the real dislocation did not come till the 890s, as Viking armies tracked across to Buttington, Chester, and Bridgnorth, from Essex. Tussling with the Vikings, Edward the Elder, the king of England, and his sister Aethelflaed, the 'lady' of the Mercians and wife of Ealdorman Aethelred, were on the offensive by 909, fortifying west midland *burhs* in the succeeding

---

[14] *Annales Cambriae*, 796, 816, 822 (= 823), 877 (= 878), 880 (= 881); *Annals of Ulster*, 877, 878. The 'A' text of the Welsh Annals calls Gwriad (who was killed in 878) Rhodri's *son*, the 'B' text calls him his *brother*.

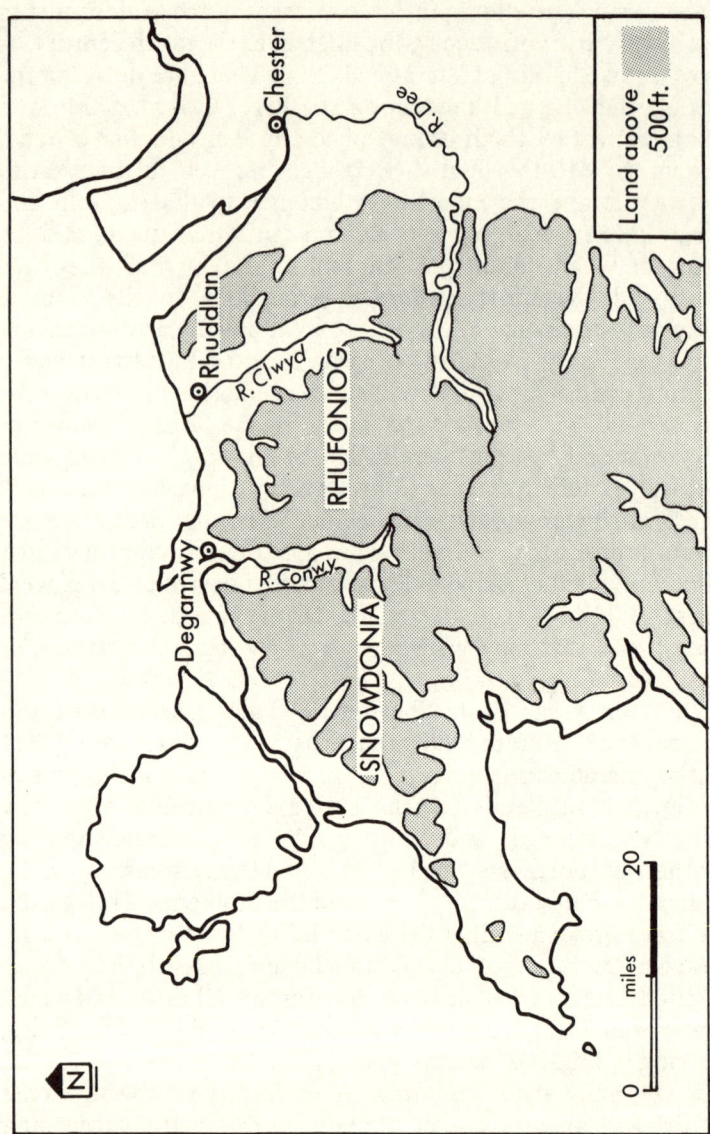

FIG. 9   The English in north Wales

decade, from Gloucestershire to Staffordshire. The greatest dislocation in the West Midlands, then, lay in the years from 893 to 919, but by the latter date Aethelflaed was dead and Edward had control of the area, the West Saxons now dominating the Mercians too. By 921 the fortification of the *burh* at Rhuddlan, at the mouth of the Clwyd, suggests that north-east Wales west to the Clwyd must also have been controlled by the English again.[15]

The political status of Chester itself may however have fluctuated: refortified by the English in 907, the townsmen (some of whom may well have been Vikings) were nevertheless in alliance with the Welsh in 924 against Edward the Elder, who died nearby at Farndon-on-Dee in that year, presumably trying to resolve the problem. There may have been a deal of instability about Chester until the death of Idwal of Gwynedd in 942, at the hands of the English, and even this did not free the area from the odd Viking attack, like the ravaging of Cheshire of 980.[16] However, once the English had re-established themselves in Chester, it seems to have been for the next hundred and fifty years or so the appropriate administrative centre for areas we *now* call north-east Wales; in 1086 Domesday Cheshire included the Welsh hundred of Atiscros (Englefield) west of the Dee to the Clwyd (see Fig. 10).[17] In other words, in the course of the tenth century—probably in the second quarter—the English regularized administration of parts of north-east Wales, organized from Chester. Some residents of this area, as of Chester itself, must have been Scandinavian, some English, and some Welsh. The Englishness of the government was no bar, however, to the city's rapidly developing commercial connections with the Scandinavian communities of Dublin and the Irish Sea

---

[15] *Anglo-Saxon Chronicle*, 865 through to 919, 921. For Rhuddlan as the site of *Cledemutha* see J. Manley, 'The Late Saxon Settlement of *Cledemutha* (Rhuddlan), Clwyd', in *Studies in Late Anglo-Saxon Settlement*, ed. M. L. Faull (Oxford, 1984).

[16] *Anglo-Saxon Chronicle*, 907, 924, 980; *Annales Cambriae*, 943 (= 942); William of Malmesbury, *De Gestis Regum*, 1. 144–5, sect. 133 (his comment, sect. 131 (p. 142), that Athelstan forced Idwal to give up his kingdom, as also King Constantine of the Scots, but then restored it, is uncorroborated).

[17] See Thacker, *VCH Chester*, 1. 248; also Lewis, 'English and Norman Government', 141–3. See below, n. 27.

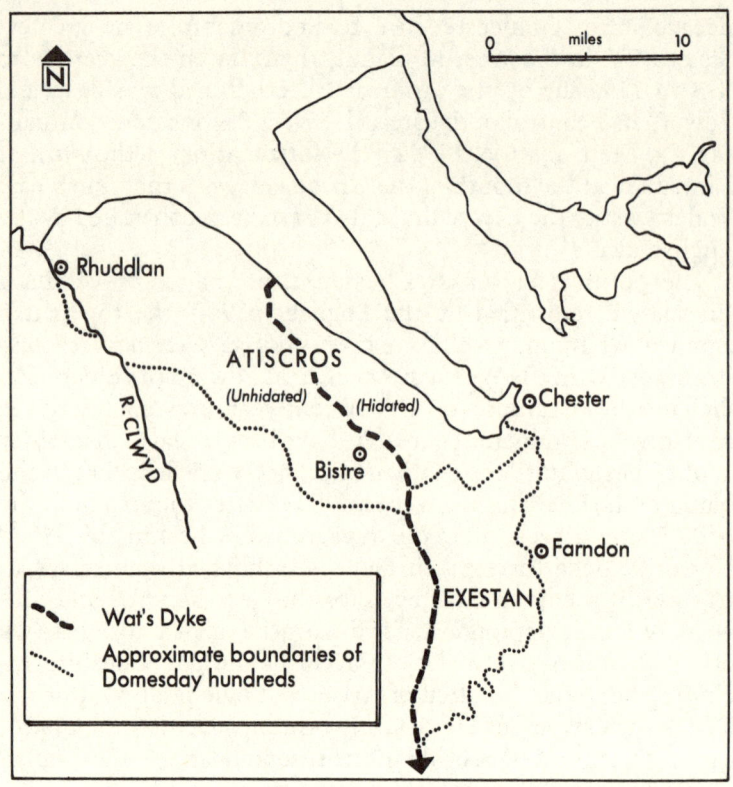

Fig. 10   West Cheshire in 1086

zone—in effect a multicultural city with a multicultural hinterland.[18]

Though the area administered from Chester stretched into north-east Wales, it must be acknowledged that it did not stretch far into Wales: in effect much of the area campaigned over in the ninth century was given up—conceded to Welsh and Vikings. Wat's Dyke, the northern extension of Offa's Dyke, in fact becomes much more meaningful as a political boundary of

[18] As Gaelic, Scandinavian, and English moneyers' names in Chester demonstrate; see Thacker, *VCH Chester*, 1. 257; ibid. 256 on integration; see further above, p. 54.

some point in the tenth century; it makes little sense at any time up to 881; it is surely unlikely that it was constructed in the period 881–907, for resources were too much needed elsewhere; it first makes sense in association with the fortification of Chester and organization of the surrounding area, that is *c*.910. It is conceivable that it was made then, but if so it must have been superseded by 921. There is no reason why it should not have been created and superseded, although other occasions in the tenth century are also potentially appropriate for its construction (in the 930s or 940s against the Welsh, in the 970s or 980s against the Vikings, for example). Whichever, it is unlikely that the Dyke constituted a final boundary: Chester still looked to the Clwyd in 1086, and had a weak west of Clwyd perspective too.[19]

ENGLISH ALLIANCES

Historians of both Wales and England have pointed to the appearance of Welsh kings at the English royal court in the second quarter of the tenth century, a period when the state of England was recognizably taking shape. English campaigning in the north and west involved some attempt to achieve the 'submission' of rulers beyond the kingdom, as of Viking leaders as they encountered defeat within England. This process had already begun in the late ninth century with King Alfred: his 'lordship', *dominium*, was accepted firstly by the southern Welsh kings (and finally by Anarawd of Gwynedd) in return for his protection from their enemies. Anarawd promised obedience

---

[19] *Domesday Book* (Cheshire), fos. 268–9. It is tempting to try and relate the construction of Wat's Dyke to the hidation of part of Atiscros, since it forms the western boundary of the hidated portion; however, as Alan Thacker points out (*VCH Chester*, 1. 267), the hidation of Cheshire was certainly reassessed more than once before the Conquest of 1066. The Domesday record is a guide to the mid-eleventh century, not to the unrecorded tenth century. It is also tempting to suppose that unhidated parts of west Cheshire must have been Welsh parts, and hidated English; however, unhidated Bistre was formerly English episcopal property. These temptations need to be resisted; the administrative history of this area clearly went through a series of changes in the tenth and eleventh centuries; the detail of most of these changes is lost. (For Wat's Dyke see further above, n. 8)

to Alfred on the same terms as had Ealdorman Aethelred of the Mercians.[20] The reciprocal nature of the arrangement is explicitly described, and might be compared—for example—with the description of relationships between Charles the Bald of West Francia and the Breton leader Salomon in the early 860s.[21] English sources thereafter record formal 'submissions' on a few occasions in the tenth century: 918 at Tamworth, 927 at Eamont (near Penrith), and rather differently 973 at Chester; it is also implied that the Welsh had submitted to the Mercians Aethelflaed and Aethelred before 918. The early tenth-century occasions were *not* submissions extracted after military campaigns to Wales and they took place in England: in other words, they do not seem to have been physically enforced (although the threat of enforcement was presumably in the background, and may be said to have overcome Idwal of Gwynedd and his son (or brother) in the end, both killed by 'Saxons' in 942). We must suppose that the Welsh kings voluntarily made the journeys to England and attended the English court; Hywel (and his brother Clydog) of Dyfed, Owain of Gwent, and Idwal of Gwynedd, were all involved in the early tenth-century submissions. Sometimes joined by other kings, like Morgan of Glywysing/Morgannwg, or Tewdwr of Brycheiniog, the presence of some of them is also recorded at a number of transactions at different English locations—Exeter 928, Worthy (Hampshire) 931, Luton 931, Winchester 934 shifting to Nottingham ten days later, Dorchester 935, Kingston-on-Thames 946 at Eadred's coronation, together with some unlocated spots (932, 949, 955, 956).[22] The series then stops—or one might see the meeting at Chester in 973 as the end of the series: in the picturesque language of the early

---

[20] *Asser's Life of King Alfred*, ch. 80; cf. H. Loyn, 'Wales and England in the Tenth Century', *Welsh History Review*, 10 (1980–1), 286. Arguably, the process had begun in 853, *Anglo-Saxon Chronicle*, 853.

[21] Asser: 'subdiderat imperio . . . ut dominium et defensionem ab eo pro inimicis suis haberent; . . . se regis dominio . . . subdidit, ut in omnibus regiae uoluntati sic oboediens esset.' For Brittany, see W. Davies, *Small Worlds*, 19–20, and J. M. H. Smith, *Province and Empire: Brittany and the Carolingians* (Cambridge, forthcoming).

[22] For detail of the charters see Loyn, 'Wales and England', *Welsh Hist. Rev.*, 10 (1980–1). For doubts about the location of the 'Eamont' meeting, see M. Lapidge, 'Some Latin Poems as Evidence for the Reign of Athelstan', *Anglo-Saxon England*, 9 (1981), 91–2.

twelfth century, Iago and Hywel of Gwynedd, Scandinavian, and northern kings rowed King Edgar on the Dee in some ceremony of submission, whether or not it was literally meant or some colourful symbolization of ship or other service demanded.[23] However, this occasion was different from the earlier ones: it took place on or near the border of Edgar's kingdom, not at a normal court within the kingdom where normal business was carried out; Edgar went there by sea—the Chronicle says he took his fleet to Chester; the kings involved were northern/north-western—north Welsh, Manx, Scots, north British; and the (in Welsh terms more powerful) *southern* kings of Wales were not involved.[24] It was not so much the end of the era but a new kind of statement; foreign policy rather than internal politics. The period of Welsh 'submission' to English kings lasted essentially from the 880s to the 950s; although revived in the mid-eleventh century, with the submission of Gruffudd ap Llywelyn in 1056 and of his half-brothers Bleddyn and Rhiwallon on his death in 1063, both these occasions came after vigorous English campaigns to Wales.[25]

The practical consequences of this relationship were presumably both a demand for tribute and the expectation of Welsh military support on English expeditions, whether regular or irregular. If William of Malmesbury—a very late witness—is to be trusted, it was certainly expected c.927, when a meeting between King Athelstan and the north Welsh, in the town of Hereford, is reported to have agreed to provision per annum of 20 lb. of gold, 300 lb. of silver, 25,000 oxen, as well as hounds and hawks. The poem *Armes Prydein* (of the mid-tenth century) implies that *some* tribute was going to England, in fact to Cirencester where the tribute-takers sat. On the other hand, northern Welsh tribute seems regularly to have gone to Scandinavians in the second half of the tenth and early eleventh

---

[23] *Anglo-Saxon Chronicle*, 973; Florence of Worcester, *Chronicon ex Chronicis*, 1. 142.

[24] The southern kings were Morgan of Glywysing/Morgannwg (though now presumably very old), Owain of Dyfed, and Owain's son Einion; it is just possible that the unknown *Iuchil* of Florence of Worcester's list is some otherwise unidentified king of the south.

[25] *Anglo-Saxon Chronicle*, 1056, 1063.

centuries.[26] The payment of tribute is certainly required by the *Anglo-Saxon Chronicle's* entry for 1063: '[Bleddyn and Rhiwallon] gave hostages to the king [Edward] . . . promising that they would . . . pay such dues from that country as had been given before to any other king.' However, there is very little to suggest the actual taking of tribute by *the English* from Wales as a whole in the century *c*.950–1050.[27]

As for military support, Welsh troops joined the West Saxon and West Midland levies who followed the Essex host to the Severn in 893, laid siege to it for several weeks at Buttington, and then defeated it. Idwal of Gwynedd, Hywel of Dyfed, and Morgan of Glywysing started for Scotland in 934, with the party that moved from Winchester to Nottingham and then north, and Hywel himself or some of his troops assisted Edmund in Strathclyde in 944/5.[28] A century later the Welshmen of Archenfield/Ergyng owed military service to the sheriff, for the English king, forming the vanguard on expeditions to Wales (though this is a local, customary obligation on members of the English kingdom, rather than the outcome of a political relationship between two powers).[29] This evidence is not detailed, but it is suggestive that the Welsh provided military levies for English campaigns at least in the 880s–950s. The *price* of submission for the Welsh rulers, therefore, was a deflection of resources and military capacity to England and with that some loss of their control of their own fighting forces.

[26] See above, p. 59; William of Malmesbury, *De Gestis Regum*, 1. 148, sect. 134 (cf. Lapidge, 'Some Latin Poems', *Anglo-Saxon England*, 9 (1981)); cf. *Anglo-Saxon Chronicle*, 927 (see also Loyn, 'Wales and England', *Welsh Hist. Rev.*, 10 (1980–1), 286–8); *Armes Prydein*, lines 69–72.

[27] The English had given lands beyond the Dee to Gruffudd, either in 1046 or 1056; the lands are not specified, though they seem to have included the bishop's lands (restored to him in or before 1063). Despite *Domesday Book's* insistence that some of these had never paid tax, it seems unlikely that the bishop's lands had not at least in theory done so, even if given a beneficial exemption, *Domesday Book* (Cheshire), fos. 263, 269; cf. Thacker, *VCH Chester*, 1. 262–3, 273. Harold had established himself in southern Gwent and started building at Portskewett by 1065, collecting movables there (and presumably local renders), *Anglo-Saxon Chronicle*; see further below, p. 86 n. 18; see also Davies, *Conquest, Coexistence, and Change*, 26.

[28] *Anglo-Saxon Chronicle*, 893; Loyn, 'Wales and England', *Welsh Hist. Rev.*, 10 (1980–1), 293–4; cf. D. Kirby, 'Hywel Dda—Anglophil?', *Welsh Hist. Rev.*, 8 (1976–7), 5; Roger of Wendover, *Chronica, sive Flores Historiarum*, ed. H. O. Coxe (London, 1841–2), 1. 398.

[29] *Domesday Book* (Hereford), fo. 179b.

In the later period, some English sometimes fought *for* the Welsh, in Wales (as Scandinavians did too): Anarawd already had English assistance against the men of Ceredigion and Ystrad Tywi in 895 (though this is a very early example); in 983 Hywel ab Ieuaf worked with Earl Aelfhere to ravage Brycheiniog and the lands of Einion ab Owain;[30] nine years later, Einion's son Edwin ravaged Maredudd's regions in the south-west (Dyfed, Ceredigion, Gower, Cydweli) with another *dux Anglorum* and took hostages; and Gruffudd ap Llywelyn worked with English dissidents in the mid-eleventh century. With Earl Sweyn (of the Wessex Godwine family) he marched into south Wales in 1046 and took hostages; nine years later he gave shelter to the outlawed Earl Aelfgar of Mercia and his Irish supporters; and together they then attacked Hereford (later Aelfgar's son Edwin had Welshmen with him when he and his brother Morcar met Earl Harold at Northampton).[31]

This practice of raising troops from any group that would do a deal, for whatever motive, constitutes a major change in the conduct of politics in Wales. It must also have had socio-political implications for relationships *within* Wales: military clientship had been extremely important for leaders, who had for centuries raised warbands to fight for glory, and generous gifts if lucky; if a 'top' ruler no longer relied on a warband of clients for military support, this must have weakened the quality of the personal military relationship, and done so before the personal relationship had a chance to become territorialized, as was happening in many parts of Europe in this period. Further, in so far as clients had tended to be Welsh, this must mean that the 'top' ruler lost touch with the natural source of supply for his warband—the local young nobles, of fighting age. In simple terms, rulers must have lost touch with their bases, although the base still had its own military capacity. Perhaps accordingly, we can also observe action taken by groups of 'leading men' in Wales, unassociated with any kings: Einion ab Owain, grandson of Hywel Dda, was killed by the 'men' of

---

[30] *Brut y Tywysogyon*, 978, assigns Saxon mercenaries to Hywel; long ago Lloyd, *History of Wales*, 351 n. 116, argued that this was an error for 'Gentiles', as *Annales Cambriae*, MS C, implies. I have assumed here and above (ch. 4) that he was right.

[31] *Annales Cambriae*, 894 (= 895), 983, 992; *Anglo-Saxon Chronicle*, 1046, 1055, 1065.

Gwent in 984, no leader named; later Gruffudd ap Llywelyn's personal retinue was attacked by the 'men' of Ystrad Tywi, no leader named.[32] Sometimes the ruler even seems to have lost touch with his personal retinue: rulers were twice killed by these retinues in the eleventh century, Iago by his own men in 1039 and Gruffudd ap Llywelyn by his in 1063.[33]

So, while the thrust of English aggression remained a problem for many Welsh, nevertheless in the tenth and eleventh centuries some Welsh leaders at some periods could ally with English kings or other English. Whether they did so by taking themselves to England or by introducing English fighters to Wales, the 'alliance' had repercussions on the military basis of power in Wales.

The long-term consequences of this complex Welsh/English interaction were, I think, major. We have underestimated the constancy of English attacks on Wales throughout the early middle ages and many have ignored the long period of English political control of north and north-east Wales, notable through the ninth century: the English were *at* Wales and *in* Wales. In the later ninth century the relationship and the interaction with the English changed, through submissions, and alliances, and making war together, whether in Wales or in England. Contacts seem to have been especially close—the closest we come to subjection of Welsh leaders to English—in the period from the 880s to the 950s, the period of the rise of the West Saxon dynasty, and of its transformation of Wessex into the extremely well-run kingdom of England. This was also, of course, the period when the English kings were struggling with the Scandinavian presence in England and with a Viking kingdom at York. As long as Scandinavians controlled northern England, the West Saxon dynasty seems to have been concerned to develop its relationships with Welsh leaders and it is in this period that we may reasonably suppose that tribute and military assistance were given. However, once the kingdom of York was secured to Eadred in 954, interest in the Welsh became less keen, border relationships apart. Memories of submission and tribute certainly

---

[32] *Brut y Tywysogyon*, 984; *Annales Cambriae*, 1047.
[33] *Annals of Ulster*, 1039; *Annales Cambriae*, 1063; *Anglo-Saxon Chronicle*, 1063.

lived long enough to be revived in the mid- and later eleventh century, when the chroniclers wrote as if Edward and his earls believed all Wales subject, and kings by right English appointees; hence fidelity, tribute, and military service due. But this was a late revival. We have little that suggests a genuinely dependent relationship in the intervening century.[34]

English contacts, however, had made their mark in many areas. Welsh books left Wales to feed the English cultural revival of the tenth century; English governmental and legal practice may have marked the formulation of some parts of the Welsh law texts and even occasionally influenced their terminology; in the South-East some people began to use English names for some of their offspring.[35] But there were things of political consequence for Wales, as well. As we have seen, military dependence, together with Scandinavian interaction, provoked some shift in the military basis of power in Wales: Welsh rulers lost control of some of their troops and lost personal touch with others. 'Submission' to the English must also have raised the possibility of the internal subordination of Welsh territorial rulers, of ruler to ruler within Wales. Before the English contacts of the late ninth and early tenth centuries, there had been no overkingship structures;[36] now, as English kings sought the submission of their Welsh subkings, those subkings—kings themselves in Wales—began to seek the 'submission' of lesser rulers in Wales. Powerful ideas of ruler interdependence had been introduced.

[34] There is something to suggest, however, that the South-East sustained some contacts with English ecclesiastical circles, W. Davies, 'The Consecration of Bishops of Llandaff in the Tenth and Eleventh Centuries', *Bull. Board Celt. Stud.*, 26 (1974–6), 64–9.

[35] David Dumville's Oxford O'Donnell Lectures (still unpublished) supplied detailed evidence of the Welsh, Cornish, and Breton books assiduously collected by the English in the tenth century; M. E. Owen, 'Shame and Reparation; Woman's Place in the Kin', in *The Welsh Law of Women*, ed. D. Jenkins and M. E. Owen (Cardiff, 1980), 56 (but see D. Dumville, 'The Aetheling: A Study in Anglo-Saxon Constitutional History', *Anglo-Saxon England*, 8 (1979)); Davies, *Llandaff Charters*, 145.

[36] See above, p. 30.

6. Patterns of Power

I have deliberately set this exploration of early Welsh politics as a search for patterns, a selection of threads through the multiple, complex patterns of power that characterize most societies.[1] There are, of course, several possible patterns of explanation. I am not interested in establishing that my particular analysis is 'right' and I certainly would not claim that it is so; rather, I am concerned to insist that there are alternatives to the traditional patterns of interpretation and explanation and that it is healthy to consider them.

By the middle of the eleventh century this was the situation in Wales: landed aristocrats, with their own private military followings, might establish themselves as kings or would-be kings anywhere. Most strikingly, a member of an intrusive ruling dynasty of the South-East, Gruffudd ap Rhydderch, started ranging over the whole of south Wales; in so doing he came into conflict with another Gruffudd, Gruffudd ap Llywelyn, who originated from one of the intrusive dynasties of the South-West but established himself in north and mid-Wales (after he defeated a Mercian force near Welshpool in 1039). Meanwhile, other would-be rulers joined the contest for the South-East, where Gruffudd's line and the line of Morgan Hen *both* called themselves kings of Morgannwg till the 1070s and at least one other family (that of Nowy ap Gwriad and descendants).used royal titles in the late tenth and eleventh centuries.[2] Gruffudd ap Llywelyn killed Gruffudd ap Rhydderch in 1055, working with the exiled English earl Aelfgar, and thereafter caused considerable trouble on the English borders. Although the English earl Harold (and latterly his brother Tostig) took the field against him in 1062 and 1063, Gruffudd died in that year at the hands of his own men. Thereupon, Welsh rulers were

---

[1] Of course, in most societies power structures encompass far more aspects than those considered here; religious power is one of the most obvious.

[2] See Davies, *Microcosm*, 95–8; one Edwin ap Gwriad in the early eleventh century was also called 'king', his family uncertain (though one might make several suggestions).

appointed by Harold, acting for King Edward (the Confessor). Harold himself was soon, if not already, establishing himself in Gwent, although his buildings were burned in 1065; shortly after this the Norman Conquest began.[3]

Although this carries no necessary implications of *social* chaos or *social* instability, this is very close to political chaos. Indeed, irrespective of the problems introduced by the Norman Conquest, in 1066 prospects for the survival and development of the Welsh kingdoms did not look good.

However, the traditional pattern of explanation of early Welsh history carries us gloriously to this point: the heroes Rhodri Mawr and Hywel Dda are impressive staging posts on the road to Welsh statehood; the hero Gruffudd ap Llywelyn— 'king of all Wales'—perches on the edge of the creation of a real kingdom of Wales, he himself only thwarted by the English, his state by the Normans. These patterns are comforting, but they say more about twentieth-century identities and twentieth-century needs than about the early middle ages. There is very little that is glorious about Welsh politics of the ninth, tenth, and eleventh centuries, even according to the traditional pattern. If we adopt another pattern, we may see the development as one of increasing chaos, but it is a chaos that is capable of rational explanation, particularly in view of changes in the ninth and tenth centuries.

APPROACHES TO POWER

Though their number is limited, early medieval texts reveal some consistent assumptions about power relationships in Wales. Power over people might take the form of power over clients, or power over menials, or power over 'subjects' (and presumably also, though less well evidenced, power over the household); the first two might reasonably be called 'lordship', though to be useful the terms need qualification, in order to indicate *which* of the two is intended. Power over land was seen to have two aspects: on the one hand the rule associated with landlordship (that is, control of the profits of exploitation of the land) and on the other the rule of wider territories associated

---

[3] See Lewis, 'English and Norman Government', 118–25, for the two Gruffudds.

with ordinance-making. Both were distinct, the former proprietary, the latter not;[4] but both were conceptualized as 'rule',
which thereby inevitably had a very strong territorial basis.[5]
Rulers of both kinds necessarily had power over people, the
former over menial dependants, the latter over 'subjects' as well
as his own menial dependants, although the former as well as
the latter might also have clients. Hence, wider territorial
domination, which is usually that which translates into the
kingships of the Latin texts, necessarily involved the wielding
of all three (or four) types of power over persons and both types of
power over land. There is little to suggest any change in these
basic concepts in the pre-Conquest period.

Ideas about the interrelationship between rulers differed in
accordance with the level of ruler and did, in the end, change.
There were always many contemporary rulers (of both kinds)
and several grades of ruler. Many distinctions in grade may have
been purely status distinctions: one king may have had a higher
worth than another without any relationship between them in
practice or by implication. But there were some relationships:
landlord rulers must usually (though not necessarily) have been
subject to rulers with territorial domination, that is subject to
the ordinances of the latter. The Llandaff text 'Braint Teilo',
which has a late tenth-century base, is effectively an immunity

---

[4] The 'multiple estate' model, which it has been suggested was prevalent
throughout the early middle ages, confuses the two. The essentially fiscal basis
of the model relates to royal, not proprietary, powers; to assume it applies to
early landlordship *as well* implies a range of political powers for mere landlords
that they do not appear to have had; it is a very big assumption. For an exposition
of the model see Jones, 'Multiple Estates and Early Settlement', in *Medieval
Settlement*, ed. Sawyer; and for my detailed comments on it, Davies, *Wales*, 43–
6. The fundamental difference of my own approach lies in the fact that I will not
accept that the entire package of late medieval Welsh law text material is
applicable to the whole of the early middle ages. Of course, it is likely that some
proportion of that material derives from the early middle ages (see my comments in Davies, *Wales*, 203–5). However, it is unlikely that that proportion was
an unchanging writ through the middle ages; everything that we know about
early medieval law texts—whether English or Visigothic or Lombard or
Frankish—demonstrates development from century to century. It is phenomen-
ally unlikely, indeed incredible, that Welsh arrangements and institutions went
unchanged for six centuries. I therefore regard it as unacceptable to suppose that
the detail and the model that were very appropriate to the twelfth and thirteenth
centuries were equally appropriate to the sixth or the tenth. If we are historians
we have to allow for development, at least in the historic period. See further
below, n. 8.

[5] See above, pp. 16–17.

and thereby negatively makes this ordinance-making point: it bestows freedoms from royal powers of command on one powerful landlord.[6] There is really very little indication of what those ordinances might have included, apart from provision for short-term problems. There is also very little to suggest that the *early* territorial ruler regularly took anything from his subjects, though doubtless he tried to do so: the first credible written suggestions of local tax-taking (as opposed to rent-taking) come in the eighth century, and build up thereafter.[7] This power develops, over time. The territorial ruler's regular income came from his own dependants, his military support from his own clients (see Fig. 1). In other words, I would stress the fact that there is no *early* evidence which suggests he took the tax/tribute and military service from his landlord subjects that a later age would naturally suppose him to have done.[8] Hence, in as much as landlords were perceived as rulers, one might reasonably call the relationship of their territorial ruler to them that of 'overruler'; but he was not a lord to them (unless they also happened to be his clients); nor was he an overking.[9]

As for relationships between territorial rulers, there is little to suggest dependence relationships between them in the early centuries. These men were independent, each ruling his own

[6] Davies, 'Braint Teilo', *Bull. Board Celt. Stud.*, 26 (1974–6), 134–6.

[7] Assessment of the fiscal issue is constantly clouded by reference to renders, which were not necessarily an aspect of anything other than landlord domination.

[8] The three prongs of royal power in early European states are the power to raise tax, raise an army, and give judgments in aristocratic cases. The crux of the issue in this case is: did all early kings automatically have all three from Day One? I think not. The development of an ability to take tax as well as rent, to raise an army as well as a personal retinue, and to hold courts (even if by proxy) for those other than personal dependants or clients (including aristocracies), is fundamental to the creation and development of state power. What is interesting is not that they all had these powers, or got them, but the different processes of doing so and differing rates by which they did develop them.

[9] One could argue for overkingship, of a limited kind, if one supposed that there was *no* relationship between the territorial ruler and the landlord's clients and dependants; the very strongly territorial basis to the concept of rule inclines me against this view—it looks as if all inhabitants of the territory were 'subjects'. However, there is no direct evidence on this point. (What I understand by 'overkingship' is essentially a relationship between two rulers (A, B), such that B owes A something but B continues to operate as an independent ruler in relation to his own subjects. It is very common in early medieval societies for the matter owed to be tribute/hosting/attendance (judicial subjection was so overtly political in the early middle ages that it was not the norm).)

regnum/gwlad; if one fought and conquered another, he took his *regnum,* adding *regio* to *regio* to form a larger *gwlad;*[10] he did not become his overking, expecting tribute and military assistance thereafter but leaving him to rule his own subjects. Hence, in the South-East, in the seventh and eighth centuries, the extension of the territorial control of the king (*rex*) of Glywysing occasioned the demotion of existing *reges* within his new territory: their families survived, but their leaders became merely landlord rulers not territorial rulers (neither *reges* nor even *subreguli*).[11] Likewise, when Rhodri took Powys and Ceredigion in the mid-ninth century, the existing royal dynasties of those kingdoms seem to have lost their royal status; he became their king, not their overking.[12]

CHANGES IN APPROACH AND IN PRACTICE

This view of relationships was challenged by the ninth- and tenth-century experience; accordingly, by the eleventh century we can begin to note changes in ideas, as well as the changes in practice that are obvious. Changing ideas about rulership are evident as much in the changing terminology as in the uncertainty of the annalists about what rulership meant on the ground. Changes in the Latin texts can be tied to the period

[10] Hence, the idea that the later medieval commote or *cantref* was the successor of a single *gwlad* is difficult to accept (above, p. 21). Territorial units, coming to be known as *cantrefi,* certainly existed in the mid-eleventh century. They *may* sometimes have coincided with the *gwlad* of an early ruler but they were too small to represent the *gwlad* of a tenth- or eleventh-century ruler. In so far as regional identity was defined by *cantref,* Sir John Lloyd's *tud/cantref* equation is reasonable; but not that of *tud* and pre-Conquest *gwlad,* since by the eleventh century the object of rule was not primarily identified with reference to population groups, and was wider than population groups. The *tud/gwlad* equation could only be appropriate, if it was so, in the largely uninvestigable fifth to eighth centuries.

[11] See Davies, *Microcosm,* 93–5. Compare Stenton's classic paper on a comparable process in Anglo-Saxon England, although in that case demotion was gradual and was preceded by an overkingship phase, F. M. Stenton, 'The Supremacy of the Mercian Kings', *English Historical Review,* 33 (1918).

[12] Bartrum, *Early Welsh Genealogical Tracts,* 12: Harleian MS 3859, nos. 30, 31. In the ninth-century *Historia Brittonum,* ch. 48 envisages a Pasgen, son of Vortigern, who was allowed to rule in Builth and Gwrtheyrnion by Ambrosius, *rex inter omnes reges.* One could argue that the author had an overkingship relationship in mind here; but *Historia Brittonum* also envisages emperors; I don't think this passage could constitute evidence of the *operation* of developed overkingship structures in Wales.

*c.*950–1020, even if changes in the vernacular texts are likely to remain a subject of debate.[13] All sorts of changes in practice, however, were becoming evident before that. The increasing territorial range of rulers is noticeable already in the mid-ninth century, in the case of the kings of Gwynedd, and in the tenth and especially the eleventh centuries more generally; by this time the link between territorial rulerships and particular territories was very weak. Segmentary conflict, evident from the ninth century, became extreme in the later tenth and eleventh centuries—especially between the descendants of Rhodri Mawr, although it was by no means confined to them.[14] But changes in practice were more complicated than this: from the late ninth century Welsh rulers and Welsh people were sometimes subject to the power of intruders. The English raided, as they had done for centuries; the Vikings raided; but, more importantly, the English achieved the submission of many Welsh rulers in the period 880s–950s; and the Vikings so effectively dominated north Wales in the period *c.*960–1025 that Welsh territorial rule became impossible. Submission to the English meant not only trips abroad—to England, north Britain—but tribute and military service to them; Viking domination meant more tribute draining away, the further alienation of Welsh resources.[15] But, paradoxically, Vikings and English were also a source of military support for Welsh rulers, although this gave more occasion to alienate resources: they revealed a pool of soldiers for hire and opened up access to it. So, in the later tenth and eleventh centuries, Vikings and English also fought in Wales *for* the Welsh; territorial rulers thereby became yet more divorced from their *regna*.

These experiences are sufficient to explain the changing perceptions (though there could well be other, hidden, factors to explain this too). They may also have stimulated other changes.

---

[13] See above, pp. 11–12.

[14] See above, pp. 44–6.

[15] See above, pp. 59, 75–6. The coin hoards deposited in coastal areas of Wales, especially in the north, and all around the Irish Sea, cannot be unrelated to the tributes paid and the mercenaries hired; see D. Hill, *An Atlas of Anglo-Saxon England* (Oxford, 1981), 43, 55, 63, for some useful maps. Cf. J. R. Maddicott, 'Trade, Industry and the Wealth of King Alfred', *Past and Present*, 123 (1989), 18, who suggests silver draining from Wales to England from the 880s.

In practice territorial rulers clearly increased demands for tribute and hosting from their subjects. One can produce a good case for the development of rulers' fiscal powers in the South-East from the mid-eighth century.[16] Elsewhere, although ideas were very much in the air in the ninth century, credible evidence of tribute-taking comes from a later period. The ravagings of Anglesey that characterize the later tenth century are often associated with the taking of tribute; this must imply that by then Anglesey was effectively a tax-taking point, by whatever method and by whomever.[17] Indeed, in general, the frequency of tribute-taking and hiring soldiers in this period implies developing machinery of exploitation. By the mid-eleventh century, rulers in Tegeingl and Gwent were drawing income from those regions, although it remains difficult to distinguish this from their income as landlords.[18] The first hints of hosting obligation do not come till the eleventh century, although 'Braint Teilo' may just suggest it was there in the South-East by the late tenth: the earlier part of the text guarantees to the church and bishops of Llandaff exemption from military service to the king of Morgannwg.[19] Late in the eleventh century the Life of Cadog specifies that Gwynllŵg should be exempt, except from the obligation to send men to serve for three days and nights, with provisions, with the king; and the Domesday customs of Archenfield indicate some

[16] See Davies, *Microcosm*, 48–50, 101, and ead., *Wales*, 130. For the general processes discussed in this paragraph, see above, n. 8.

[17] See above, pp. 58–9. It is just possible that Bede's eighth-century description of Anglesey as land of 960 *familiae* is a reference to an early fiscal assessment; but there are many other possible interpretations of and approaches to this comment; *Historia Ecclesiastica*, 2. 9.

[18] See above, p. 81, and my comments in this chapter, nn. 4, 7, above. In Tegeingl, tax clearly came from hidated Atiscros; *Domesday Book* says it did *not* come from unhidated Atiscros and Bistre—and implies Gruffudd's renders at Bistre were proprietary not royal; however, see above, p. 76 n. 27. In Gwent, *Domesday Book* (Gloucestershire), fo. 162a, has a reeve with groups of vills rendering dues to the king in 1086, with an implication that there were earlier royal dues from this area; however, all groups of vills did *not* so render; see Lewis, 'English and Norman Government', 306–9.

[19] Part One (early twelfth century): 'Priuilegium sancti Teliaui est . . . libera ab omni regali seruitio . . . sine expeditione'; Part Two (*c*.950–1090): 'Y thir hay dayr dy luyd, di uuner, di gauayl' ('Its lands [shall be] without military service, tax, distraint'); Davies, 'Braint Teilo', *Bull. Board Celt. Stud.*, 26 (1974–6), 134, 135. I now think 'tax' a more likely meaning of *uuner* than 'burden' in this context.

military obligation to the *English* king, when his sheriff led expeditions into Wales.[20] These are but slight indications of development, but they *are* indications.[21]

The changing experiences may have also (as I suggested above) initiated more fundamental changes, and changes which affected relationships between rulers. Rulers and would-be rulers, now only rarely *reges*, were distanced from the regions, and from the 'men' (and 'elders') of the region, as the territories they sought to control became larger. Rulers and would-be rulers were distanced from their clients, as they tried to raise troops to fight in England and used English and Scandinavians to fight in Wales. Political society became less close-knit; political relationships more diffuse and diverse. It was a wider society and a more mobile one.[22] Prolonged submission to the English introduced new ideas: ruler dependence and the association of tribute and military service with it, a fully fledged view of

[20] *Vita Cadoci*, ch. 25; *Domesday Book* (Hereford), fo. 179b; see Davies, *Wales*, 131; Davies, *Conquest, Coexistence, and Change*, 118.

[21] We might also expect kings to have developed judicial powers (see above, n. 8); but there is not much to suggest that they had courts other than their own proprietary courts, nor aristocratic jurisdiction other than that determined by the ebb and flow of politics; contrast the role of local *degion*, 'worthies', settling the ninth-century dispute of Tudfwlch and Elgu in the 'Surexit' charter of the Lichfield marginalia, Jenkins and Owen, 'Welsh Marginalia', *Camb. Med. Celt. Stud.*, 5 (1983), 51, and 7 (1984), *passim*. I have nothing to add to the comments I made in Davies, *Wales*, 134–40, on kings, law, and order in general, though I would reiterate the point that southern law texts suggest that landowners by reason of their landownership had powers of jurisdiction, and thereby perhaps their own courts. There is little direct evidence on the matter but this may well have been so in the late pre-Conquest period too: late pre-Conquest material from the South-East certainly indicates that in the tenth and eleventh centuries landowners would hold their own courts, in which any offences against the landowner would be heard, and they claim that this was even so when committed by a person of higher status; at this period nothing suggests the existence of a hierarchy of courts. See the narrations in the later Llandaff charters, *Book of Llan Dâv*, nos. 217, 218, 222, 223, 233, 237b, 249b, 259, 261, 263, 267; *Vita Cadoci*, cc. 22, 33, 37; Davies, 'Braint Teilo', *Bull. Board Celt. Stud.*, 26 (1974–6), 134–6. There may be a reference to landowners' jurisdiction in the tenth-century 'Stanzas of the Graves' (Jones, *Proc. Brit. Acad.*, 53 (1967), 127, no. 48): '[his] justice (*gwir*) was strong in his land'; see Jenkins and Owen, *Camb. Med. Celt. Stud.*, 7 (1984), 99–100.

[22] There had been wide raiding much earlier, in the early seventh century, most obviously that associated with Cadwallon of Gwynedd in his dealings with Northumbrian and Mercian kings in England. However, everything suggests that these wide-ranging kings of the early seventh century travelled with their personal military retinues (*teulu*) and few others—small, swift-moving, and close-knit groups. It was an altogether different world.

overkingship; the perception and experience of submission must have made it an end of political relationships within Wales. In other words, having submitted to Alfred or Edward or Edgar, Welsh rulers began to seek the submission of other Welsh rulers.[23] In practice they effected military victory and demanded military assistance in further campaigns; and in practice they condoned what was to all intents and purposes independent rule of the submitting ruler within his own territory. Territorial rulers therefore became subject to territorial rulers. So, Edgar was seen as resolving a dispute between Hywel and Morgan over the extent of political spheres in the mid-tenth century;[24] Iago was seen to *hold* Anglesey of Rhydderch in the 1020s; and, like Gruffudd ap Llywelyn to Edward, Hywel was at once *subregulus* in relation to Rhydderch, and *rex* in his own right.[25]

By the eleventh century there were hardly any polities. Even less was there any sense of Welsh political identity, although use of the English term *Gualia* for 'Wales' from the mid-eleventh century indicates some consciousness of territorial identity. Despite the surprising comments of some respectable academics—that 'Welsh nationality first attained something like its modern character' in the early middle ages—the unit 'Wales' had not politically taken shape at the start of the Norman Conquest; consciousness of group identity remained essentially small-scale.[26] Expressions of horror at the arrival of the new aggressors in the late eleventh and twelfth centuries were at first related to the South-West: 'one vile Norman intimidates a hundred natives with his command, and terrifies

---

[23] James Campbell has pointed out to me that Bede suggests that the early seventh-century Welsh kings submitted to the Northumbrians; true, *Historia Ecclesiastica*, 2. 20, has Cadwallon 'rebelling' against Edwin, but *HE*, 3. 1 has him ravaging Northumbria for *a year*; it was hardly submission of the ninth- and tenth-century type; in any case, there was a long gap before the late ninth century.

[24] *Book of Llan Dâv*, no. 247; this is a corrupt text and may well represent an eleventh- rather than a tenth-century record; however, its significance for our purposes is the perspective, not the historicity of the data recorded.

[25] Ibid., no. 253 and p. 252 (a record of episcopal consecration). These examples are all south-eastern; unfortunately there is very little material from other areas to compare; however, south-eastern politics and practices were much more closely related to those of the rest of Wales in this period than they had been previously.

[26] T. Charles-Edwards, 'Some Celtic Kinship Terms', *Bull. Board Celt. Stud.*, 24 (1970–2), 122.

[them] with his look . . . the broken spirit falls, weighed down by lethargy . . . Our limbs are cut off, we are lacerated, our necks condemned to death, and chains are put on our arms'; Dewi of St David's was the presiding, protecting saint, and St David's became the archbishopric; it was only with the persistence of Norman activity that the outraged began to combine in outrage.[27]

There has not been much in this study which has gone back to the notion of Celtic kingship, although it was one of my starting-points. This or that looks Irish, especially—for example—the political powers of the land-holding aristocracy, but this or that looks English, or Scandinavian, or early Frankish; and other things are purely Welsh. Whatever similarities there may have been between the institutions of peoples speaking Celtic languages in the distant past, by the fifth century AD the experience of those peoples was so varied, the influences then bearing upon them so different, the environments surrounding them so diverse, that it is a nonsense to suppose that all Celtic societies were developing in like ways. Such similarities as there were are often characteristic of any medieval society dominated by a landed warrior aristocracy.[28] Indeed, rulership

[27] See above, pp. 19–21; Rhigyfarch's Lament, lines 19–39 (Lapidge, 'Welsh-Latin Poetry', *Studia Celtica*, 8–9 (1973–4), 88–92); see also on Welsh identity and its development in the twelfth century, R. R. Davies, 'Law and National Identity in Thirteenth-Century Wales', in *Welsh Society and Nationhood: Historical Essays presented to Glanmor Williams*, ed. R. R. Davies and others (Cardiff, 1984), 51–4.

[28] Professor Binchy's *Celtic and Anglo-Saxon Kingship* has been extremely influential in encouraging the layman to suppose that there were norms of Celtic kingship in the historic period; I am sure that he did not intend his ideas to be used in quite this way but he did try to identify similarities between Irish and Welsh kingship which it is very difficult to substantiate in practice; the models are overwhelmingly Irish and they do not have to apply outside Ireland—indeed, often do not apply at all. See, for example, the criticisms made by P. Wormald, 'Celtic and Anglo-Saxon Kingship: Some Further Thoughts', in *Sources of Anglo-Saxon Culture*, ed. P. E. Szarmach (Kalamazoo, 1986). Wormald occasionally tries to force the Welsh material into the Irish model too, but his paper is helpful in stressing that many characteristics of Irish kingship can be found in plenty of other northern European societies. While noting the general similarities, we should not suppose that everything was the same everywhere; one of our primary tasks is to distinguish between what was similar and what was different. (The Irish material is of course very important, because it is very rich and because it provides us with clear evidence of an early medieval system in which kings did not have a monopoly, even a notional monopoly, of political power; see above, p. 30 n. 49, and Davies, 'Clerics as Rulers', in *Latin and the Vernacular Languages in Early Medieval Britain*, ed. Brooks.)

in Celtic areas evidently developed in different ways: at the least rulers had different roles in relation to assemblies in the early middle ages, in relation to law, and in relation to judgment-finding.[29]

In Wales, as elsewhere in Europe, the ninth and tenth centuries were a period when directions changed. Some comparable things happened, but some of the norms of western European development did not. We do not find the territorialization of the client relationship in Wales nor labour service, until introduced from outside in the later middle ages; we do not find the governmental and administrative development necessary to support the expansionist ambitions of the pre-Conquest rulers, who preferred to rely on military alliance rather than institutional development. This clearly conditioned the long period of the Norman takeover, striking in contrast to the Norman conquest of England;[30] there was little administrative machinery to adopt, little system for them to operate.[31]

Why then was Wales 'underdeveloped'? It can hardly be accounted for by simple geography nor by its position on the periphery of the island; for that matter, the highly successful kingdom of England was peripheral, as also that of Denmark; while the mountainous regions of Scotland and of northern

[29] One might also contrast the highly developed overkingship structures of Ireland and the single monarchy that was established in Scotland; or the military capacities of Irish and Welsh rulers and absence of such among local Breton machtierns. The king's role seems to have been essential to local assemblies in Ireland but not in Wales; in Ireland professional lawyers also served as judges (as the king might do too) but in Wales (and Brittany) judgment was essentially the business of local panels of worthies: in Wales the function of law-making was separated from judgment. For Irish judges, see R. Sharpe, 'Dispute Settlement in Medieval Ireland', in *The Settlement of Disputes in Early Medieval Europe*, ed. W. Davies and P. Fouracre (Cambridge, 1986), 183–4 (though note his warnings about the king's role in this, ibid. 186–7). See too R. R. Davies, 'In Praise of British History', in *The British Isles 1100–1500*, ed. R. R. Davies (Edinburgh, 1988), 18–21, esp. n. 45, for differences between Celtic kingships in the later middle ages.

[30] See above, n. 10.

[31] See, again, Rees Davies, 'Kings, Lords and Liberties', *Trans. Royal Hist. Soc.*, 29 (1979): 'it is in the March itself, in the character and chronology of its conquest . . . in the evolution of its governance . . . that we must seek an explanation of the powers assumed by the Norman lords'; also Rowlands, 'The Making of the March: Aspects of the Norman Settlement', in *Proc. Battle Conf. 1980*, ed. Brown, 153–4; all this *pace* Edwards, 'The Normans and the Welsh March', *Proc. Brit. Acad.*, 42 (1956) (although J. G. Edwards himself made the fragmentation (*morcellement*) of Wales point, ibid. 177).

Spain supported rapidly developing monarchies.[32] Was it the failure to grasp the economic opportunity, to use and develop resources? Resources there were, but for much of the central middle ages Wales was a place to plunder: Welsh resources, like Welsh books, were scattered outside Wales. And Welsh land-lords did little to increase the exploitation of what remained— the land. Too many enemies and too many lost opportunities combined by the eleventh century to retard development. There were always people with power in early Wales, but no one ever had enough.

[32] Cf. Wormald's comments on Irish 'backwardness', in 'Celtic and Anglo-Saxon Kingship', in *Sources of Anglo-Saxon Culture*, ed. Szarmach, 170–1, and Davies's comments on Irish and Welsh 'backwardness' in 'In Praise of British History', in *The British Isles*, ed. Davies, 20–1.

List of Works Cited

PRIMARY SOURCES

Annales Cambriae, ed. J. Williams ab Ithel (Rolls Series; London, 1860). There are more recent editions of some texts or parts of texts. 'A' text: E. Phillimore, 'The "Annales Cambriae" and Old-Welsh Genealogies from "Harleian MS" 3859', *Y Cymmrodor*, 9 (1888), 141–83; 'B' and 'C' texts, 1035–93: J. E. Lloyd, Appendix to 'Wales and the Coming of the Normans', *Transactions of the Honourable Society of Cymmrodorion* (1899–1900), 165–79. (There is a translation in *Nennius: British History and the Welsh Annals*, ed. and trans. J. Morris (Chichester, 1980).) Cited throughout by year AD, as computed by modern editors, for which see *Brut y Tywysogyon*, ed. T. Jones.

The Annals of Ulster (to AD 1131), ed. S. Mac Airt and G. Mac Niocaill (Dublin, 1983). Cited by year AD, as in this edition.

The Anglo-Saxon Chronicle: a Revised Translation, ed. D. Whitelock with D. C. Douglas and S. I. Tucker (London, 1961). Cited by year AD, as in this translation.

Armes Prydein, ed. I. Williams, trans. R. Bromwich (Dublin, 1972).

Asser's Life of King Alfred, ed. W. H. Stevenson (Oxford, 1904); for translation, see *Alfred the Great*, trans. S. Keynes and M. Lapidge (Harmondsworth, 1983), 65–110.

Bede's Ecclesiastical History of the English People, ed. and trans. B. Colgrave and R. A. B. Mynors (Oxford, 1969).

Book of Llan Dâv (The Text of the), ed. J. G. Evans with J. Rhys (Oxford, 1893).

Brut y Tywysogyon, Peniarth MS. 20, ed. T. Jones (Cardiff, 1941); translation and notes in *Brut y Tywysogyon, or The Chronicle of the Princes, Peniarth MS. 20 Version*, trans. T. Jones (Board of Celtic Studies, History and Law Series, 11; Cardiff, 1952).

Brut y Tywysogyon, or The Chronicle of the Princes, Red Book of Hergest Version, ed. and trans. T. Jones (Board of Celtic Studies, History and Law Series, 16; Cardiff, 1955).

Canu Aneirin, ed. I. Williams (Cardiff, 1938); translation (and Williams's edition) in A. O. H. Jarman, *Aneirin: Y Gododdin* (Welsh Classics, 3; Llandysul, 1988). For an earlier translation, see K. H. Jackson, *The Gododdin* (Edinburgh, 1969). Cited by stanza number.

Canu Llywarch Hen, ed. I. Williams (Cardiff, 1935); see also J. Rowland, 'Saga Englynion', Ph.D. thesis (Univ. Wales, 1982), Part 2 (= vol. 3), for new text and translation (Woodbridge, forthcoming). For an earlier translation, see P. K. Ford, *The Poetry of Llywarch Hen* (Berkeley, 1974). Cited by stanza number.

Canu Taliesin, ed. I. Williams (Cardiff, 1960); translation in M. Pennar, *Taliesin Poems* (Lampeter, 1988). Cited by poem number.

Cartularium Saxonicum, W. de Gray Birch (4 vols.; London, 1885–99).

Collectio Canonum Hibernensis: see *Die irische Kanonensammlung*.

Colloquy: see Stevenson.

Críth Gablach, ed. D. A. Binchy (Dublin, 1941).

Domesday Book, seu Liber Censualis Willelmi primi Regis Angliae, ed. A. Farley (2 vols.; Record Commission, 1783).

Early Christian Monuments: see Nash-Williams.

FLORENCE OF WORCESTER, *Chronicon ex Chronicis*, ed. B. Thorpe (2 vols.; London, 1848–9).

Fragmentary Annals of Ireland, ed. J. N. Radner (Dublin, 1978).

Genealogies: see Bartrum.

GILDAS, *De excidio et conquestu Britanniae*: in *Chronica Minora saec. IV. V. VI. VII*, 3, ed. T. Mommsen (MGH AA 13; Berlin, 1898), 1–85; trans. M. Winterbottom, *Gildas, The Ruin of Britain* (Chichester, 1978).

Hen Gerddi Crefyddol, ed. H. Lewis (Cardiff, 1931).

Historia Brittonum: in *Chronica Minora saec. IV. V. VI. VII*, 3, ed. T. Mommsen (MGH AA 13; Berlin, 1898), 143–222.

Historia Gruffud vab Kenan, ed. D. Simon Evans (Cardiff, 1977); for translation, see *The History of Gruffydd ap Cynan*, ed. and trans. A Jones (Manchester, 1910).

IEUAN: see Lapidge, 'Welsh-Latin Poetry'.

Die irische Kanonensammlung, ed. F. W. H. Wasserschleben (2nd edn.; Leipzig, 1885).

The Irish Penitentials, ed. L. Bieler (Dublin, 1963).

JONES, T., 'The Black Book of Carmarthen "Stanzas of the Graves" ', *Proceedings of the British Academy*, 53 (1967), 97–137.

Liber Landavensis: see *The Book of Llan Dâv*.

RHIGYFARCH: see Lapidge, 'Welsh-Latin Poetry'.

ROGER OF WENDOVER, *Chronica, sive Flores Historiarum*, ed. H. O. Coxe (4 vols.; English Historical Society, London, 1841–2).

STEVENSON, W. H. (ed.), *Early Scholastic Colloquies* (Anecdota Oxoniensia, Med. and Mod. Series, 15; Oxford, 1929).

STOKES, W., 'The Welsh Glosses and Verses in the Cambridge Codex of Juvencus', 'The Old-Welsh Glosses at Oxford', *Transactions of the Philological Society* (1860–1), 204–49, 288–93.

—— 'The Old-Welsh Glosses on Martianus Capella, with Some Notes on the Juvencus-Glosses', *Beiträge zur vergleichenden Sprachforschung*, ed. A. Kuhn, 7 (Berlin, 1873), 385–416.

Trioedd Ynys Prydein, ed. and trans. R. Bromwich (Cardiff, 1961).

Vita Cadoci: in *Vitae Sanctorum Britanniae et Genealogiae*, ed. A. W. Wade-Evans, 24–140.

Vita Samsonis: in *La Vie de S. Samson*, ed. R. Fawtier (Paris, 1912).

Vitae Sanctorum Britanniae et Genealogiae, ed. and trans. A. W. Wade-Evans (Cardiff, 1944).

WILLIAM OF MALMESBURY, *De Gestis Regum Anglorum libri quinque*, ed. W. Stubbs (2 vols.; Rolls Series 90; London, 1887–9).

OTHER WORKS

BAILEY, R. N., *Viking Age Sculpture in Northern England* (London, 1980).

BARTRUM, P. C. (ed.), *Early Welsh Genealogical Tracts* (Cardiff, 1966).

BASSETT, S. (ed.), *The Origins of Anglo-Saxon Kingdoms* (London, 1989).

BINCHY, D. A., *Celtic and Anglo-Saxon Kingship* (Oxford, 1970).

BLACKBURN, M., and PAGAN, H., 'A Revised Check-List of Coin Hoards from the British Isles, c. 500–1100', in *Anglo-Saxon Monetary History: Essays in Memory of Michael Dolley*, ed. M. A. S. Blackburn (Leicester, 1986), 291–313.

BOON, G. C., *Welsh Hoards 1979–81* (Cardiff, 1986).

CAMPBELL, J., JOHN, E. and WORMALD, P., *The Anglo-Saxons* (Oxford, 1982).

CHARLES, B. G., *Old Norse Relations with Wales* (Cardiff, 1934).

CHARLES-EDWARDS, T. M., 'Some Celtic Kinship Terms', *Bulletin of the Board of Celtic Studies*, 24 (1970–2), 105–22.

—— 'Native Political Organization in Roman Britain and the Origin of MW *brenhin*', in *Antiquitates Indogermanicae*, ed. M. Mayrhofer, W. Meid, B. Schlerath, R. Schmitt (Innsbruck, 1974), 35–45.

CLARKE, J. E., 'Welsh Sculptured Crosses and Cross-slabs of the Pre-Norman Period', Ph.D. thesis (2 vols.; University College London, 1981).

COPLESTONE-CROW, B., 'The Dual Nature of the Irish Colonization of Dyfed in the Dark Ages', *Studia Celtica*, 16–17 (1981–2), 1–24.

CRAWFORD, B. E., *Scandinavian Scotland* (Leicester, 1987).

DAVIES, R. R., 'Kings, Lords and Liberties in the March of Wales, 1066–1272', *Transactions of the Royal Historical Society*, 29 (1979), 41–61.

—— 'Law and National Identity in Thirteenth-Century Wales', in *Welsh Society and Nationhood: Historical Essays presented to Glanmor Williams*, ed. R. R. Davies and others (Cardiff, 1984), 51–69.

—— *Conquest, Coexistence, and Change: Wales 1063–1415* (Oxford, 1987).

—— 'In Praise of British History', in *The British Isles 1100–1500:*

Comparisons, Contrasts and Connections, ed. R. R. Davies (Edinburgh, 1988), 9–26.

DAVIES, W., 'Braint Teilo', *Bulletin of the Board of Celtic Studies*, 26 (1974–6), 123–37.

—— 'The Consecration of Bishops of Llandaff in the Tenth and Eleventh Centuries', *Bulletin of the Board of Celtic Studies*, 26 (1974–6), 53–73.

—— *An Early Welsh Microcosm* (London, 1978).

—— *The Llandaff Charters* (Aberystwyth, 1979).

—— 'Property Rights and Property Claims in Welsh "Vitae" of the Eleventh Century', in *Hagiographie, cultures et sociétés*, ed. E. Patlagean and P. Riché (Études augustiennes; Paris, 1981), 515–33.

—— 'Clerics as Rulers: Some Implications of the Terminology of Ecclesiastical Authority in Early Medieval Ireland', in *Latin and the Vernacular Languages in Early Medieval Britain*, ed. N. Brooks (Leicester, 1982), 81–97.

—— *Wales in the Early Middle Ages* (Leicester, 1982).

—— 'Celtic Women in the Early Middle Ages', in *Images of Women in Antiquity*, ed. A. Cameron and A. Kuhrt (London, 1983), 145–66.

—— *Small Worlds: The Village Community in Early Medieval Brittany* (London, 1988).

DODGSON, J. McN., 'The English Arrival in Cheshire', *Transactions of the Historic Society of Lancashire and Cheshire*, 119 (1967), 1–37.

DOLLEY, R. H. M., 'The Pattern of Viking-Age Coin-Hoards from the Isle of Man', *Seaby's Coin and Medal Bulletin* (1975), 296–302, 337–40.

—— 'The Palimpsest of Viking Settlement on Man', in *Proceedings of the Eighth Viking Congress: Århus, 24–31 August 1977*, ed. H. Bekker-Nielsen, P. Foote, O. Olsen (Medieval Scandinavia Supplements, 2; Odense, 1981), 173–81.

DUMVILLE, D. N., 'Some Aspects of the Chronology of the *Historia Brittonum*', *Bulletin of the Board of Celtic Studies*, 25 (1972–4), 439–45.

—— 'The Corpus Christi "Nennius" ', *Bulletin of the Board of Celtic Studies*, 25 (1972–4), 369–80.

—— ' "Nennius" and the *Historia Brittonum*', *Studia Celtica*, 10–11 (1975–6), 78–95.

—— Review of Hughes's 'Welsh Latin Chronicles', *Studia Celtica*, 12–13 (1977–8), 461–7.

—— 'The Aetheling: A Study in Anglo-Saxon Constitutional History', *Anglo-Saxon England*, 8 (1979), 1–33.

—— 'The "Six" Sons of Rhodri Mawr: A Problem in Asser's *Life of King Alfred*', *Cambridge Medieval Celtic Studies*, 4 (1982), 5–18.

—— 'Brittany and "Armes Prydein Vawr" ', *Études Celtiques*, 20 (1983), 145–59.

EDWARDS, J. G., 'The Normans and the Welsh March', *Proceedings of the British Academy*, 42 (1956), 155–77.

EDWARDS, N., 'A Possible Viking Grave from Benllech, Anglesey', *Anglesey Antiquarian Society and Field Club Transactions* (1985), 19–24.

—— and LANE, A. (eds.), *Early Medieval Settlements in Wales AD 400–1100* (Bangor and Cardiff, 1988).

FELLOWS-JENSEN, G., 'Scandinavian Settlement in the Isle of Man and North-West England: The Place-Name Evidence', in *The Viking Age in the Isle of Man*, ed. C. Fell, P. Foote, J. Graham-Campbell, R. Thomson (London, 1983), 37–52.

FINBERG, H. P. R., *The Early Charters of the West Midlands* (Leicester, 1961).

—— *Lucerna* (London, 1964).

FLEURIOT, L., *Dictionnaire des gloses en vieux bretonne* (Paris, 1964; rep. Toronto, 1985).

FOX, Sir C., *Offa's Dyke: A Field Survey of the Western Frontier-Works of Mercia in the Seventh and Eighth Centuries A. D.* (London, 1955).

GELLING, M., 'The Early History of Western Mercia', in *The Origins of Anglo-Saxon Kingdoms*, ed. Bassett, 184–201.

GRABOWSKI, K., and DUMVILLE, D., *Chronicles and Annals of Mediaeval Ireland and Wales* (Woodbridge, 1984).

GRAHAM-CAMPBELL, J., 'Some Viking-Age Penannular Brooches from Scotland and the Origins of the "Thistle-Brooch" ', in *From the Stone Age to the 'Forty-Five*, ed. A. O'Connor and D. V. Clarke (Edinburgh, 1983), 310–23.

—— 'The Viking-Age Silver Hoards of the Isle of Man', in *The Viking Age in the Isle of Man*, ed. C. Fell, P. Foote, J. Graham-Campbell, R. Thomson (London, 1983), 53–80.

—— 'Two Scandinavian Disc Brooches of Viking Age Date from England', *The Antiquaries Journal*, 65 (1985), 448–9.

—— 'Tenth-Century Graves: The Viking-Age Artefacts from the Peel Castle Cemetery and their Significance', in D. Freke, *Peel Castle Excavations, 1982–7*, forthcoming.

HILL, D., *An Atlas of Anglo-Saxon England* (Oxford, 1981).

—— 'Offa's, Wat's, and Shorter Dykes', *Medieval Archaeology*, 25 (1981), 184–6; ibid. 30 (1986), 150–3.

—— 'The Construction of Offa's Dyke', *The Antiquaries Journal*, 65 (1985), 140–2.

HOLM, P., 'The Slave Trade of Dublin, Ninth to Twelfth Centuries', *Peritia*, 5 (1986), 317–45.

HUGHES, K., 'British Museum MS. Cotton Vespasian A. xiv (*'Vitae Sanctorum Wallensium'*): Its Purpose and Provenance', in N. Chadwick and others, *Studies in the Early British Church* (Cambridge,

1958), 183–200; reprinted in her *Celtic Britain in the Early Middle Ages* (Woodbridge, 1980), 53–66.

HUGHES, K., 'The Welsh Latin Chronicles: *Annales Cambriae* and Related Texts', *Proceedings of the British Academy*, 69 (1973), 3–28; reprinted in her *Celtic Britain in the Early Middle Ages* (Woodbridge, 1980), 67–85.

JACKSON, K., *Language and History in Early Britain* (Edinburgh, 1953).

JENKINS, D., 'Kings, Lords, and Princes: The Nomenclature of Authority in Thirteenth-Century Wales', *Bulletin of the Board of Celtic Studies*, 26 (1974–6), 451–62.

—— *The Law of Hywel Dda* (Welsh Classics, 2; Llandysul, 1986).

—— and OWEN, M. E., 'The Welsh Marginalia in the Lichfield Gospels, Pt. 1', *Cambridge Medieval Celtic Studies*, 5 (1983), 37–66; 'Pt. 2, The "Surexit" Memorandum', ibid. 7 (1984), 91–120.

JOHN, E., *Orbis Britanniae and Other Studies* (Leicester, 1966).

JONES, G. R. J., 'Post-Roman Wales', in *The Agrarian History of England and Wales*, 1, pt. 2, ed. H. P. R. Finberg (Cambridge, 1972), 281–382.

—— 'Multiple Estates and Early Settlement', in *Medieval Settlement*, ed. P. H. Sawyer (London, 1976), 15–40.

KIRBY, D., 'Hywel Dda—Anglophil?', *Welsh History Review*, 8 (1976–7), 1–13.

KNIGHT, J. and others, 'New Finds of Early Christian Monuments', *Archaeologia Cambrensis*, 126 (1977), 60–73.

KOCH, J. T., 'The Cynfeirdd Poetry and the Language of the Sixth Century', in *Early Welsh Poetry: Studies in the Book of Aneirin*, ed. B. F. Roberts (Aberystwyth, 1988), 17–41.

KRUSE, S., 'Ingots and Weight Units in Viking Age Silver Hoards', *World Archaeology*, 20 (1988), 285–301.

LAMBKIN, B. K., 'The Structure of Sacred and Secular Lordship in the Poems of Blathmac', MA thesis (The Queen's University, Belfast, 1985).

LANE, A., 'The Vikings in Glamorgan?', in *Glamorgan County History*, 2, ed. H. N. Savory (Cardiff, 1984), 354–6.

LAPIDGE, M., 'The Welsh-Latin Poetry of Sulien's family', *Studia Celtica*, 8–9 (1973–4), 68–106.

—— 'Some Latin Poems as Evidence for the Reign of Athelstan', *Anglo-Saxon England*, 9 (1981), 61–98.

—— 'Latin Learning in Dark Age Wales: Some Prolegomena', in *Proceedings of the Seventh International Congress of Celtic Studies, Oxford, 1983*, ed. D. E. Evans, J. G. Griffith, E. M. Jope (Oxford, 1986), 91–107.

—— and DUMVILLE, D. N. (eds.), *Gildas: New Approaches* (Woodbridge, 1984).

LEWIS, C. P., 'English and Norman Government and Lordship in the Welsh Borders, 1039–87', D.Phil. thesis (University of Oxford, 1985); publication forthcoming, Oxford.

LEWIS, J. M., 'Recent Finds of Penannular Brooches from Wales', *Medieval Archaeology*, 26 (1982), 151–4.

LLOYD, J. E., *A History of Wales from the Earliest Times to the Edwardian Conquest* (2 vols.; London, 1911).

LOYN, H. R., *The Vikings in Wales* (London, 1976).

—— 'Wales and England in the Tenth Century: The Context of the Athelstan Charters', *Welsh History Review*, 10 (1980–1), 283–301.

MADDICOTT, J. R., 'Trade, Industry and the Wealth of King Alfred', *Past and Present*, 123 (1989), 3–51.

MANLEY, J., 'The Late Saxon Settlement of *Cledemutha* (Rhuddlan), Clwyd', in *Studies in Late Anglo-Saxon Settlement*, ed. M. L. Faull (Oxford, 1984), 55–64.

MAUND, K. L., 'Cynan ab Iago and the Killing of Gruffudd ap Llywelyn', *Cambridge Medieval Celtic Studies*, 10 (1985), 57–65.

NASH-WILLIAMS, V. E., *The Early Christian Monuments of Wales* (Cardiff, 1950).

NIERMEYER, J. F., *Mediae Latinitatis Lexicon Minus* (Leiden, 1976).

Ó CORRÁIN, D., 'Irish Regnal Succession: A Reappraisal', *Studia Hibernica*, 11 (1971), 7–39.

O'RAHILLY, C., *Ireland and Wales: Their Historical and Literary Relations* (London, New York, etc., 1924).

Ó RIAIN, P., 'The Irish Element in Welsh Hagiographical Tradition', in *Irish Antiquity: Essays and Studies Presented to Professor M. J. O'Kelly*, ed. D. Ó Corráin (Cork, 1981), 291–303.

OLSEN, B. L., and PADEL, O. J., 'A Tenth-Century List of Cornish Parochial Saints', *Cambridge Medieval Celtic Studies*, 12 (1986), 33–71.

OWEN, M. E., 'Shame and Reparation; Woman's Place in the Kin', in *The Welsh Law of Women*, ed. D. Jenkins and M. E. Owen (Cardiff, 1980), 40–68.

POLY, J.-P., and BOURNAZEL, E., *La Mutation féodale, x^e–xiie siècles*, (Paris, 1980).

PRETTY, K., 'Defining the Magonsaete', in *The Origins of Anglo-Saxon Kingdoms*, ed. Bassett, 171–83.

PRYCE, H., 'Early Irish Canons and Medieval Welsh Law', *Peritia*, 5 (1986), 107–27.

REYNOLDS, S., 'Medieval *Origines Gentium* and the Community of the Realm', *History*, 68 (1983), 375–90.

—— *Kingdoms and Communities in Western Europe, 900–1300* (Oxford, 1984).

ROWLAND, J., 'A Study of the Saga Englynion, with an Edition of the

Major Texts', Ph.D. thesis (3 vols.; University of Wales (UCW Aberystwyth), 1982); forthcoming publication, Boydell and Brewer, Woodbridge, as *The Welsh Saga Englynion*.

ROWLANDS, I. W., 'The Making of the March: Aspects of the Norman Settlement in Dyfed', in *Proceedings of the Battle Conference on Anglo-Norman Studies, 3, 1980*, ed. R. A. Brown (Woodbridge, 1981), 142–57.

SAWYER, P. H., *Anglo-Saxon Charters: An Annotated List and Bibliography* (London, 1968).

—— *The Making of Sweden* (Alingsås, 1988).

SHARPE, R., 'Gildas as a Father of the Church', in *Gildas: New Approaches*, ed. Lapidge and Dumville, 193–205.

—— 'Dispute Settlement in Medieval Ireland', in *The Settlement of Disputes in Early Medieval Europe*, ed. W. Davies and P. Fouracre (Cambridge, 1986), 169–89.

SHERINGHAM, J. G. T., 'Les Machtierns: Quelques témoignages gallois et cornouaillais', *Mémoires de la société d'histoire et d'archéologie de Bretagne*, 58 (1981), 61–72.

SMITH, F. G., 'Talacre and the Viking Grave', *Proceedings of the Llandudno, Colwyn Bay and District Field Club*, 17 (1931–3), 42–50.

SMITH, J. M. H., *Province and Empire: Brittany and the Carolingians* (Cambridge, forthcoming).

STENTON, F. M., 'The Supremacy of the Mercian Kings', *English Historical Review*, 33 (1918), 433–52.

—— *Anglo-Saxon England* (3rd edn.; Oxford, 1971).

THACKER, A. T., 'Anglo-Saxon Cheshire', in *A History of the County of Chester*, 1, ed. B. E. Harris with A. T. Thacker (The Victoria History of the Counties of England, Oxford [for the Institute of Historical Research, London], 1987), 237–92.

WAINWRIGHT, F. T., 'Ingimund's Invasion', *English Historical Review*, 63 (1948), 145–69.

WHITE, R. B., 'Excavations at Arfryn, Bodedern', *Anglesey Antiquarian Society and Field Club Transactions* (1971–2), 19–51.

WILLIAMS, I., *The Beginnings of Welsh Poetry*, ed. and trans. R. Bromwich (Cardiff, 1972).

WOOD, I. N., 'Forgery in Merovingian Hagiography', in *Fälschungen im Mittelalter, Internationaler Kongress der Monumenta Germaniae Historica, München, 16–19 September 1986* (5 vols.; Hanover, 1988), 5. 369–84 (= MGH Schriften, 33. 5).

WORMALD, P., 'Celtic and Anglo-Saxon Kingship: Some Further Thoughts', in *Sources of Anglo-Saxon Culture*, ed. P. E. Szarmach (Studies in Medieval Culture, 20; Kalamazoo, 1986), 151–83.

Index